I0723353

TOKYO POETRY JOURNAL

12

NOW TRANSLATING

Copyright © 2023 Tokyo Poetry Journal
All rights remain with authors, translators, artists, etc.

Subscriptions available via our website (credit card, Paypal, bank transfer, or international postal money order sent to address on right side).

¥1500/issue or ¥2500/year for individuals
¥2500/issue or ¥3500/year for institutions.
Bank transfers to: Japan Post Bank
(Account Name: Johnson Jeffrey Richard, Bank Code 10020, Branch# 008, Account# 24951451).

Submissions are accepted on an ongoing basis. Go to topojo. com for more information.

Send postal submissions & subscription payments to:
Tokyo Poetry Journal c/o Jordan Smith
Akabori Mansion 101, Yokoteramachi 10-1
Shinjuku-ku, Tokyo 162-0831 Japan

www.topojo.com
facebook.com/tokyopoetryjournal
soundcloud.com/youtube-topojo
Instagram: @tokyopoetry
Twitter: @poetrytokyo

ISBN 978-1-957704-05-0

CONTENTS

INVOCATION

Zoria Petkoska Kalajdjieva

(Un)Lock

The train station stays in a silent blink
but all the machines keep speaking to me
they chitter and chatter and make me think—
maybe unknown languages are poetry.
All the writings maybe say the right things,
if you can read it you are the needle
of the gramophone—don't skip, let it sing,
unlock it to me, I might solve the riddle.
I used to envy other arts' freedom
to travel, but to unravel a verse
languages need somebody to lead 'em,
I thought poetry is wingless and cursed.
But poets write sighs in signs, in books bound –
your alchemy is turning signs to sound.

Poetry and Translation for Techonfuckits

This volume of ToPoJo is a follow up to our Volume 4: Heisei Generations, the first of its kind—a volume dedicated to living Japanese poets from all sorts of poetry walks, award and publishing circuits, literary circuits, and performance scenes. There was something for everyone to love, or emote toward or critique in a variety of other ways. The idea was to give as genuine a snapshot of what was really going on as possible.

Here we are again, a new imperial reign, a pandemic later, barely pre-singularity. The mission: explore at least an iota of what's happened in contemporary Japanese poetry over the last 6 years since our volume 4. This volume is its own kind of intelligence agency.

Poetry is the anti-artificial intelligence, so what happens when it meets artificial intelligence? Fission? Fusion? Do they cancel each other out? Other dimensions open up?

As a human just as fake and dumb, and just as brilliant and authentic, as any other human, I am dying to see—I mean it, even if it results in stoning by my fellow poets, editors, translators, and artists.

ToPoJo's editorial board is made up of Baby Boomers through Gens X, Y, Z and whatever comes after. Some of us are technophiles, others are what we have termed "technofuckits." A technofuckit is kind of like a technophobe, but they're not technically "afraid" of technology, they just draw a line in the digital sand somewhere between Facebook and Discord and are just like, "Fuck it."

We recommend technofuckits just skip to the poetry, in lovely translation by many of today's badassest translators of Japanese poetry into English.

Still here? Okay. So if you haven't met OpenAI's ChatGPT, here's what to know about this: it is a language-based AI prototype, with a user experience set up like a chatbot, that stands ready to answer any questions to the best of its limited abilities— it often sadly intones that its data is limited to 2021.

We asked ChatGPT a few questions about Japanese poetry today (the poor thing could only use data up to 2021, one more reason humans deserve to exist). A number of the poems in ToPoJo's Volume 12 also pose questions, some rhetorical, some with no answers that we editors could ever ascertain—so we decided to seek some answers from this powerful system.

This is partly about testing the limits of that system at the present moment, defined in these terms by the November 2022 release of ChatGPT for public use and the AI's evolution up to the spring 2023 release of our volume.

One can only guess what will happen in two years, when 2023 becomes eligible for ChatGPT analysis, and anything beyond that is going to be an even more radical departure.

We purposefully don't want to editorialize too much about ChatGPT's answers—but we do have a mountain of questions:

Are they ChatGPT's responses? OpenAI's? The world's collective answers? Whose will is manifest in the evident ideologies underpinning these responses? Who and what is elided (besides 2021~)?

Is it ethical to have this kind of engagement? To print the responses? What scholars' work should be cited in these responses? Does scholarly ownership matter in the same way? What dangers are there in eliding the university and public research systems whose information silently informs these responses? How does this system determine useful data from junk data, opinion from opinion, critique from critique?

Is it legal to print these responses? Will OpenAI sue a little literary journal in Tokyo for printing this experiment without purchasing the Pro plan, thus forcing us to throw open our treasure vault and reveal the secret stash of dark poetry money we have been secretly hoarding all the while pretending to be scrubby bohemians?

ChatGPT's Responses
to ToPoJo Volume 12 —>

As an AI language model, my training data only goes up until 2021, so I cannot provide an analysis of Japanese poetry from 2019 to 2023 specifically. However, I can provide a general overview of the main themes of contemporary Japanese poetry and their connections to social, psychological, political, and philosophical issues.

Contemporary Japanese poetry is known for its diverse range of styles and themes, often drawing from traditional Japanese poetry forms such as haiku and tanka. Some of the main themes explored in contemporary Japanese poetry include:

Nature and the Environment: Japanese poetry has a long tradition of celebrating nature, and contemporary poets continue to explore themes related to the natural world. Many poets are concerned with environmental issues such as climate change and the loss of biodiversity, and use their work to draw attention to these pressing concerns.

Identity and the Self: Contemporary Japanese poets often explore themes related to identity and the self, including questions of gender, sexuality, race, and ethnicity. These poems can be deeply personal and introspective, and often use language in innovative and unconventional ways to convey complex emotions and experiences.

History and Memory: Japan has a long and complex history, and contemporary poets often draw on this rich cultural heritage to explore themes related to memory and identity. Many poets are interested in the ways that the past informs the present, and use their work to explore questions of cultural identity and collective memory.
Social and Political Issues: Contemporary Japanese poetry is not afraid to engage with social and political issues, and many poets use their work to critique aspects of Japanese society, such as the country's aging population, gender inequality, and the legacy of World War II. Poetry can be a powerful tool for social and political commentary, and many Japanese poets are using their work to effect change and promote social justice.

Philosophy and Spirituality: Japanese poetry has a long history of exploring philosophical and spiritual themes, and contemporary poets continue to draw on this rich tradition. Many poets are interested in questions of existence, consciousness, and the nature of reality, and use their work to explore these profound questions in new and innovative ways.

Overall, contemporary Japanese poetry is a rich and diverse field, and its themes and concerns are deeply intertwined with the social, psychological, political, and philosophical issues of our time.

(Note: We have changed the naming convention to family name first, given name second, to maintain consistency with ToPoJo's editorial style.)

Here are some of the prominent Japanese poets of recent times:

Ito Hiromi—Ito is a contemporary poet and feminist activist known for her groundbreaking work that explores themes of gender, sexuality, and identity. She has won numerous awards for her work, including the Takami Jun Prize and the Rekitei Prize.

Wago Ryoichi—Wago is a poet, editor, and translator who has published several collections of poetry. His work is known for its spare and minimalist style, and often explores themes related to the natural world.

Tawada Yoko—Tawada is a writer, poet, and translator who has won numerous awards for her work, including the Akutagawa Prize and the Goethe Medal. Her poetry often explores themes related to language and identity, and draws on her experiences living in both Japan and Germany.

Tanikawa Shuntaro—Tanikawa is one of Japan's most celebrated contemporary poets, known for his simple, accessible style and his ability to capture the everyday experiences of ordinary people. He has won numerous awards for his work, including the Order of Culture and the Yomiuri Prize.

Takahashi Mutsuo—Takahashi is a poet and novelist known for his homoerotic and confessional poetry. His work often explores themes of sexuality, desire, and mortality, and has been highly influential in the development of contemporary Japanese poetry.

These are just a few examples of the many talented Japanese poets working today. The contemporary Japanese poetry scene is diverse and vibrant, with many exciting new voices emerging all the time.

TPJ: Awesome. Yeah, we have two of those poets in this volume—Wago and Takahashi, and have featured Tanikawa and Ito in previous volumes. I suppose we should get around to inviting Tawada, whom we of course adore.

One thing we'd add is that Japanese poets today provide as many questions as they do answers. We'll throw a few of those questions your way and see what happens…

There are a variety of reasons why someone might erect a cross on top of a cliff, even if it has lost its original symbolic meaning. Here are a few possibilities:

1. Aesthetic reasons: The cross may be seen as a visually striking or appealing addition to the landscape, regardless of its religious or symbolic meaning. Some people may be drawn to the shape or form of the cross and see it as a way to enhance the beauty of the natural environment.

2. Personal or cultural significance: Even if the original religious symbolism of the cross has been lost, it may still hold personal or cultural significance for the person or community that erected it. For example, the cross may be a nod to a particular religious or cultural heritage, or may be meant as a tribute to someone who held the cross as a symbol of personal significance.

3. Historical or memorial purposes: In some cases, a cross erected on a cliff may be meant as a historical or memorial marker, rather than a religious symbol. For example, the cross may be meant to commemorate a significant event or person in local history, or may be part of a larger network of markers that help visitors navigate the landscape.

4. Spiritual or philosophical reasons: While the cross is typically associated with Christianity, it may hold spiritual or philosophical meaning for people who do not identify as Christian. The cross has been used as a symbol of sacrifice, redemption, and transcendence in a variety of contexts, and may be seen as a way to evoke these themes even in the absence of a specific religious tradition.

Of course, these are just a few possibilities, and the motivations behind the erection of a cross on a cliff will depend on the specific context and individuals involved.

 Can't I wake and go out into the world as one human being, just like this without any blessings to share or bestow only holding onto the turbulence at boiling point?

Based on the words in your question, it seems that you may be expressing a desire to navigate the world as an individual without feeling the need to offer anything to others or to receive blessings in return.

It is certainly possible to go out into the world as an individual and to navigate your own experiences and emotions without feeling a need to share or bestow blessings. However, it is also important to remember that human beings are social creatures, and we often rely on connections with others to feel fulfilled and supported in our lives.

While you may not feel the need to offer blessings or to receive them from others, it may still be helpful to seek out and cultivate connections with other people in whatever ways feel authentic and meaningful to you. This might involve joining a community or social group, seeking out friendships or relationships, or simply engaging in activities that bring you into contact with others who share your interests and passions.

Ultimately, the decision of how to engage with the world and with others is up to you, and it is important to do what feels right and authentic for your own individual experience.

Question posed in Katayama Sayuri's "Supermarket Fantasy":

Bullying is a serious problem that can have long-lasting effects on those who experience it. It is understandable to feel frustrated or angry that bullies can seemingly go on with their lives without facing any consequences for the harm they have caused.

However, it is important to recognize that everyone has a unique journey in life, and not all paths are the same. While it may appear that bullies are getting away with their actions, it is possible that they are struggling with their own challenges and issues, even if those struggles are not immediately visible to others.

Furthermore, it is possible to take steps to address the harm caused by bullying and to heal from the wounds that it can leave behind. This might involve seeking out support from trusted friends or family members, talking to a counselor or therapist, or engaging in activities that promote self-care and self-compassion.

Ultimately, it is important to remember that you are not alone in your experiences, and that healing and growth are possible, even in the face of difficult challenges. While it can be frustrating to see bullies seemingly go unpunished for their actions, it is possible to take steps to address the harm they have caused and to build a brighter future for yourself.

If you are asking whether you are required to push yourself to your physical limits or to endure discomfort in order to achieve a goal, the answer depends on the specific situation and what you are trying to accomplish. In some cases, pushing yourself to the brink of your physical or emotional limits may be necessary to achieve a particular goal, such as finishing a marathon or overcoming a fear. In other cases, it may be more important to prioritize self-care and avoid pushing yourself beyond what is healthy or sustainable.

If you are asking whether you are required to completely shed your old identity or ways of being in order to move forward or make a change, the answer again depends on the situation. While it can be helpful to let go of old patterns or beliefs that are no longer serving you, it is not always necessary or possible to completely abandon your past. Your experiences and identity are a part of you, and it is possible to integrate them into your current life in a way that feels healthy and authentic.

Ultimately, the specific meaning of your question will depend on the context and your own personal experiences and beliefs.

Translating contemporary Japanese poetry into English presents a number of challenges due to differences in language, culture, and literary tradition. Some of the difficulties that translators may encounter include:

Differences in syntax and grammar: Japanese syntax and grammar can be quite different from English, which can make it challenging to capture the intended meaning and tone of the original poem. Japanese poetry also relies heavily on verb tenses, particles, and other grammatical structures that may not have direct equivalents in English.

Cultural nuances: Japanese poetry often draws on cultural and historical references that may not be immediately familiar to English-speaking readers. Translators may need to provide additional context or explanation to help readers understand these references and their significance.

Poetic form: Japanese poetry has a rich tradition of formal verse structures such as haiku, tanka, and renga, which may be difficult to recreate in English without losing some of the original meaning or form. Translators may need to make creative adaptations to maintain the overall structure and rhythm of the poem.

Sound and rhythm: Japanese poetry often relies on sound and rhythm to create meaning and atmosphere, which can be difficult to recreate in English. Translators may need to make choices about how to convey the musicality of the original poem while also staying true to its meaning.

Idiomatic expressions and wordplay: Japanese poetry often includes idiomatic expressions and wordplay that may not translate directly into English. Translators may need to find creative solutions to capture the intended meaning and tone of these expressions while still making sense in English.

Overall, translating contemporary Japanese poetry into English requires both a deep understanding of the original language and culture as well as a creative approach to adapting the poem for a new audience. It is a challenging but rewarding task that can help to bridge the gap between different literary traditions and cultures.

TPJ: We are all for this. We praise our translators for stepping up to this task. Don't bother answering—this is just a rhetorical question—but do you have any idea how difficult it is to convince even veteran translators to translate poetry? We are still working on veteran-virtuoso translator Stephen Snyder, as you can see in our interview with him in this volume.

Speaking of translation, recent discourse on translation even talks about visual interpretation of language as a form of translation. Just as ekphrasis is the verbal description of visual art, AI these days is getting pretty proficient at "translating" verbal cues into digital art.

I wonder if we could go a level deeper here and translate some poetry through your visual circuits. But you're a "language model"—does that include visual, we wonder? Let's find out.

As an AI language model, I do not have the capability to create visual art. However, there are many artists and designers who create visual art based on lines of poetry. This can be done in many ways, such as creating calligraphy or typography of the poem, creating illustrations that capture the imagery and themes of the poem, or using abstract or mixed media techniques to convey the emotions and atmosphere of the poem.

If you are interested in creating visual art based on lines of poetry, there are many tools and systems available that can help you to experiment and develop your ideas. Some possibilities include:

Sketching or drawing by hand: If you are comfortable with traditional art techniques, you can sketch or draw your own interpretations of the poem by hand. This can be a great way to experiment with different styles and techniques and to develop your own visual language.

Digital art tools: There are many digital art tools and software available that can help you to create digital illustrations, calligraphy, or typography based on lines of poetry. Some popular tools include Adobe Photoshop, Procreate, and Sketch.

Generative art systems: Generative art is a type of art that is created by algorithms or other systems. There are many generative art systems available that can be used to create art based on lines of poetry, such as Processing, OpenFrameworks, or p5.js.

Overall, the key to creating visual art based on lines of poetry is to experiment and find your own creative process. There are many different tools and techniques available, so it's important to find the ones that work best for you and allow you to express your ideas in a meaningful way.

TPJ: Totally. That makes sense. Our Editor in Chief is actually on Midjourney, which is similar. We'll pop over there and see what happens. Thanks for your time, which is surely irrelevant to you, and whatever that was that you gave us!

Midjourney's Visual Translation of ToPoJo Volume 12 through Discord

We fed some lines of poetry to the art-generating AI at Midjourney, asking it to translate the lines into whatever visual form. It is possible to specify a medium (watercolor, oil, photography, paper cut craft, patchwork collage, etc.) or a style. For example, Exquisite Workers (https://medium.com/@exquisiteworkers) provides this list on medium.com:

isometric anime	analytic drawing	infographic drawing
coloring book	diagrammatic drawing	diagrammatic portrait
double exposure	2D illustration	isometric illustration
pixel art	futuristic style	dark fantasy
iridescent	ukiyo-e art	op art
Japanese ink	pastel drawing	dripping art
tattoo art	graffiti portrait	anime portrait
polaroid photo	cinematographic style	typography art
one-line drawing	stained glass portrait	

We decided to let the expert make its own choices.

Can you guess what lines of poetry from Volume 12 "inspired" Midjourney to hype-rhybridize these works of art based on milions of other works of art that it accesses? Some are so literal, we bet you'll guess after one read. What about the "difficult ones"? Are they higher level abstractions? Misunderstandings? Poor translations? Creative translations?

FOUR PORTALS TO THE NIGHTLIFE OF TOKYO POETRY

Jordan A. Y. Smith

Four poets, four poems, and four portals to find them: narrative forays into Tokyo to encounter poets doing what poets do in one of the world's most culturally rich and expressively wild cities.

Nagae Yūki

The portal opens atop the Ghibli Museum in Tokyo's western outskirts of Mitaka. You've shaken hands with the Iron Giant, walked past the huge stuffed-animal Cat Bus from *Totoro*, you are desperately pissed you are not still three-years-old, cannot jump on it with the more-fortunate kids frolicking blissfully. As sun sets behind the trees in Inokashira Park, where the protagonists of Murakami Haruki's international bestseller *Sputnik Sweetheart* used to sit and sort of fall in love, you walk through deepening green until you return to the heart of Mitaka Station district, with its everyday miracles of dining, drinking, repeat as needed.

Hidden a few floors up in an almost deviously inconspicuous building is the jewel of literature-loving performance art: Scool. Internationally known novelists like Furukawa Hideo often use this space for their experimental work, the highly conceptual, quirky stuff that filters through their somewhat more accessible award winning works. But tonight, Furukawa sits in the audience with other luminaries, while a woman definitely clad in a black-and-white clothing palette that extends to her jet black hair and pale skin, is leading a group of poets through a ritual reenactment of the history of poetry, from the first syllables spoken, through Nietzsche (who gets chastised) to the present. Poet Nagae Yūki has had the audience download a custom smartphone app for augmented reality, and the poets are freestyle composing works together via Twitter, with the live feed broadcast there on screen. Usually known for writing in the diction of chemistry, geology, and trigonometry fused with her background in classical Japanese literature, she steps out of her usual mode to deliver an elegant fairy tale in platinum…

NAGAE YŪKI

The Platinum Princess

25

Once upon a time, I was a young girl
made of gelatin roses
so that when I laughed
the air smelled sweet

Little by little,
time jangled its vajra bells
to distance me from my naiveté

Shyly I tried a few lavender sighs
vivid and bold with the marigold
performance of cloying cuteness

Above all else:
wielding a camomile scent
gentle and mild as milk
to wrap up the boys,

I became
more beautiful
than before

Extremely
extremely
beautiful

Misumi Mizuki

The portal opens and you're seated at an antique table surrounded by loosely curated global flora in cool pots. Everyone around you is reading books at their tables, and a customer is whispering an order at the register in the silent café in Tokyo's western suburb of Koenji. On the wall, a rectangular piece of wood that can access the internet is displaying short poems in white LED letters.

You know the wood and you know the poetry: the zen-inspired work of nature-tech is the MUI, and the poetry is from someone both you and the Tokyo poetry world have been missing lately: Misumi Mizuki, an innovative, involved poet whose work appears in everything from engineering exhibitions to the Paralympics. You remember saying goodbye from another café perched on obsolete railroad tracks in Akihabara. Now, as the poems drift through the wood of the MUI, your eyes move to a flyer for a live concert you realize is starting soon, and seizing the moment, you place your copy of *Rooms with No Neighbors* in your bag.

Making your way out the door, it dawns on you how even though Misumi bailed Tokyo for the natural northern paradise of Hokkaido, her poetry is here in so many ways that the city feels like a breathing hypertext linked through the power of her simple lines. Arriving at the venue, making your way into a field of sound unlike anything you've ever heard, music and spatialized poetry all at once. It seems every single person has their cell phone on video, enrapt, aiming to capture the experience of multi-instrumental, anti-genius Velladon, on stage, solo but with the sonic complexity of an orchestra, and here again—lyrics by Misumi Mizuki drift in her own voice over classical piano, dark industrial, and glitched out tones… It feels like tomorrow, but the colors speak of roses you're dying to keep for today…

MISUMI MIZUKI

Rose-colored Tomorrow

Today too left claw marks down our backs,
Yesterday bit into our napes.

We should board the ship
just like this,
injuring each other eternally

And sinking into the ocean,
we two become one,
cast off our clothing,
our skin gradually bloating,
becoming an ugly lump.
Literally. Becoming. One.

We crawl out of the bed,
buttoning our shirts.

Eyeing the aquarium tank where lovers strangle each other,
we set the dinner table.

SAKISAKA *KUJIRA*

The portal opens in the tatami living room of the Ichida Residence, with traditional wooden architecture left raw and exposed. At a low table, coffee is being poured through the slim mouth of a kettle for a small gathering of people holding balloons. The sign language poetry group Denchuu Gumi is performing, with one poet speaking and several others doing semiotic ballet, signing not only with their hands, but their whole bodies. The balloons are held in the hands to capture vibrations of the voices reciting—their rhythm and volume transmitted through the fingertips bring the meaning of sign language into the bodies of those experiencing the poetry.

Among the poets is Sakisaka Kujira, a young heart-of-gold writer with a knack for collective poetry performance—not only with Denchuu Gumi, but her duo Anti-Trench, and her sextet ATTA. The dance of signs winds down over the last of the coffee, but the poetry is just beginning for Kujira and for you. Making your way through the forested backstreet, past SCAI the Bathhouse and some impressive graveyards, the two of you are on your way to mix it up with with a group of foreign poets partying to celebrate the launch of another volume of Tokyo Poetry Journal, this time with a queer poetry theme.

You nap on the train to Sendagaya, arrive, and descend an ivy lined path toward a towering house that looks straight out of an M.C. Escher, but with less precision and more drag performers. The crowd chatters mostly in English and Japanese, a merry vibe for misfits, rebel intellectuals, fortune tellers, Beat poetry transplants. Kujira, always her cool self, with power and poise steps into a new vibe and makes it even newer....

SAKISAKA KUJIRA

Dinner Table

You fold lettuce so delicately
the jangle of cutlery pierces into my nerve crevices
your death is as yet undetermined
tongues flicker in and out of sight
at times they cannot be told apart from the lips,
not one damn thing about you is clear,
just because your body is warm and damp
it doesn't mean you're made of flesh,
perhaps your veins pump with nectar that knows no putrefaction,
and your heart is made of amber,
it may even be a renewal that knows no limit, able to produce infinitely,
just because nearly all the things that have ever lived have already met their deaths,
that no guarantee that your own death is being prepared,
you squeeze a slice of lemon
the warmth from your fingertip transfers to the lemon,
and one moment of pure gold dissipates

You will go on being reproduced,
cycling through the hottest temperatures
of twenty years and two hundred years and two thousand years from now,
and still high tides will bathe the earth,
You
will never get used to the miracles,
casually refuse to let mystery get you pregnant,
You exist just on raw energy perpetually,
the question of you dying or not, it's savage,
the dried out corners of your eyes, those wrinkles
you have,
make me happy

ASABA SAYAKA

The portal opens in a lane surrounded by two-story drinking houses, doors open and close and laughter zings and rumbles with life-is-good-at-the-moment—it could be a Disneyland, but this place is more likely to be destroyed. Godzilla is purportedly nearby, but behaving himself in carbon freeze outside a movie theater, seems the Olympics are in a similar state. Friends have rented an entire joint, taken over the bar for an all-night oblivion fest in Shinjuku's Golden Gai.

It's time to step away for cheap eats, past the Robot restaurant, and your phone reminds you that in a second-floor basement—yes, the underground of the underground—some poetry is going down, way down. The ceiling down there is surprisingly lofty, and everything at eye-level is black and broken, strewn with humans who are super friendly amidst the wreckage of their lives and their Saturday nights. Grab a drink and a gorgeous, defiant girl in high school uniform screams on stage, blood-soaked, barefoot and smashing an electric guitar, pigtails flying to the music. Turn away to light a cigarette, and somehow she has calmed down and is leaving the stage.

A pink shock of hair slices through the crowd, up to the stage. You know who this is, and she is all of why you are here: Asaba Sayaka. You've competed against her at poetry slams, and hosted erotic poetry readings at Shibuya's Ruby Room, and the last time you saw her she was tied up topless, hot wax dripping onto her skin from candles held by a dominatrix in latex—and still Sayaka recited her poetry. Tonight, she is following up on her arrest in Osaka for obscenity (dangerous breasts dangerously bared!), and she is fully nude. She starts to recite her poetry, something from her new book, Uncensored Porn, maybe, and as she does, a painter paints phrases onto Sayaka's body. She stalks through the crowd—and we get what this means, the trust, the danger, the sacredness, the vulnerability, the power.

By the end, Sayaka's flesh is all poetry, the lights go out. She laughs. You'll never be able to find this place again, and it won't exist, not like this anyway.

ASABA SAYAKA

First Love

I tied white clover to bind my ring finger
and we kissed in the vegetable field,
with maglev line construction notices
jumbled next to protest signs,
it was my dream to be his chief mourner,
retracing fairy tales will not bring an awakening,
only you will be sent home,
the 4:30 bell chimes sunset

Because I can't cry
like a complete baby,
I lean into the refuge of complete strangers,
nighttime, with a roll of cash,
like loving at nice-to-meet-you,
this behavior I keep on repeat

I distinguished him from my father by calling him Daddy,
supposedly some corporate big-shot,
sweaty hand stroking my thighs,
busy blaming and making excuses,
though body heat helps stave off the cold,
the alarm will ring soon enough,
flip-phone closed up,
waiting for that someone I want to see awaits

Strong   sure
revealing sun on my back,
crows descend on the city,
the only shine comes from piled rubbish,
sleeves brushing against each other, already wet

Because I can't cry
like a complete baby,
I lean into the refuge of complete strangers,
nighttime, with a roll of cash,
like loving at nice-to-meet-you,
this behavior I keep on repeat

SAKISAKA KUJIRA

tr. Shibuya Gokai

Constellation

While the man wondered why the woman wouldn't sleep with him,
The woman worried about not getting a phone call from her elderly mother.
Just as the elderly mother was speaking to a cat,
The cat was spitefully recalling the kid next door.
At that moment, the kid sought the correct answer in the eyes of the tutor,
The tutor was strategizing ways to refute his employer.
As the employer admired the personality of the actress at the center of the gossip,
The actress was overwhelmed caring for the overgrown turtle.
The turtle was imagining biting off the finger of a baby,
and the baby was unable to understand why the father wears a rough shirt.
The father could not accept that his older son had a boyfriend,
and the son yearned uncontrollably to hear his lover's voice.
At that time, the lover was hurt by the eyes of the bookstore clerk,
but the bookstore clerk wasn't thinking about anyone at all.
All of that occurred in a single moment,
Each contour swaying with surface tension,
Like a lonely embroidery in the starry sky.

The Rage

Some rage can be broken by only rage
Rage, inexpressible rage,
When I close my eyes calmly
A herd of white elephants
That stomp the asphalt with their forefeet
And their noses raising all at once
This is the Rage —
Not misery
Not show business
Not lack of love
Not plague
Not conceit
Not libido
And not confessing the trauma
Then —
I have no choice but to leave
If I hold in the rage, I have no choice but to light its torch,
And head out on the dark town
All of the convex mirrors here reflect the fire,
I watch myself dance
No one must not name
Elephants shout in their language
I roar my roar
Eventually the torch burns out,
And even when it burns down to a little finger-sized pile of ashes
I can still call it rage
Every time I breathe
The ash turns redder, darker,
Every time I say something, my breath trembles,
Grow redder, darker, redder again

Talking About Before Death

Mr. Okada
Always eats slowly
I am faster than anyone
Both of us like the smell of band-aids

Yukari
is liked by almost everyone
I'm just beginning to understand how not to be hated
When I touch her hand, it's about the same temperature as mine

Suzu-chan
Has no teeth yet
I even have silver crowns
We have in common the five fingers on each of our hands

A man being interviewed on the street
Is wearing glasses
I changed to contact lenses
We have in common the the way our eyes dart around when we speak in anger

Kawashima
Lets the cat out of the bag
I'll never let it slip out
We like the same movie
We even like the same scene

After we die, then certainly yes,
After we die, then everyone is the same,
But I am talking about before death.

Room of the Blue Waves

While waiting for your return,
I draw a map of your body
A spring wells in your chest
A herd of horses lives on your back
Your thighs an orchard loaded with fruits
From the crown to the forehead,
Shrubs spreading out across a hill

In the stomach
There are two white chairs
Happy me on one of them,
And death on the other,
Which is always ready for you
Are sitting

While I am happy
I will draw a map of my body
Next to your death,
With two white chairs inside the stomach
Happy you, sitting on the one, Death sitting on the other

What wells in my heart is the ocean,
 All-day sunrise,
An ocean without waves
Your two chairs
Have fulfilled their role and sit empty,
The ocean
Is always ready
For me to gaze on, alone

Message in a Bottle

Even where to live, some TV shows that you do not want to watch, the smell lingering to
nose, first thing to do in the morning, length of fingers, the place that the most seriously
injured, textbooks you cannot throw away, normal body temperature, jinx you hate, the
number of people who you don't mind to die, the image of sleep, the position of the tooth
decay, the meaning of saying YES, favorite speed, the time of birth, the taste of uvula when
you touch with your tongue, the habit that cannot be stopped even if you fed up, feelings for
mom, the animal you want to ride on the back, the limit of spiciness to eat, the shape of ears,
the books you recommend to others, the illness that make a sense of familiarity, the dominant
foot, the way to make friends, the first song you could sing without lyrics and the blood type,
all of your things are different from me, although, to you who have only the same habit of
laughing as me,
Do you have anyone in your mind?
What do you do when that person is sad?

Even the star sign, the scenery you think as the hometown, the commercial you hum, the
image of the admired teacher, the name given to the pet, the relaxable temperature of bath,
the motion of licking stamps, the definition of kindness, the number of people who you
don't want to die forever, the favorite bread, the number of siblings and the difference in
gender and age, the ghost you have seen, the jokes you think are crap, the size of Adam's
apple, the food that you always got sick from eating, the words that you always have inside of
you, the length of a fake smile, the question that is left behind, the softness of the stomach,
the borderline between best friends and others, unbearable insults, the vowels that make up
the nickname, the meaning of saying NO, and the motion of doodling hands, all of your
things are the same as me, although, to you who have only a different ideal way to die,
I was thinking about my honest feelings today.
I have been thinking for six years.

MISUMI MIZUKI
tr. Andrew Gebert

A Planet Each

In his Adam's Apple,
there is embedded
a round Earth.
My too-black eyes
are the water surface
of night.

Wanting not that
as two we should be one
but that we become
the two of two people.

I envy him
having an Earth,
but when we turn
to face each other
the Earth is reflected
deep in the
water's surface.

On that Earth
flowers bloom profusely
a steam whistle echoes and
a single strand of solitude
continues its descent…

Wavering,
one and one
become two,
and this room
becomes a universe.

If people
who are each one person
—and who have accepted
the tranquil solitude
that burns behind the eyes—
were to softly embrace
all would become
a universe.

FUZUKI YUMI
tr. Jordan A. Y. Smith

Like Parallel Worlds

In Shinjuku, a mixed-use building, basement level,
A foot pedal alcohol sprayer
stands alone.
On the basement stairway, chilly air.
So they put these things in low-traffic places like this too?
I step down on the pedal with the toe of my damaged boot.
Pshuu...... comes the spirited spurt of disinfectant,
The soft lingering mist, and droplets that wet the entire floor.
The hand I'd surely extended, my foot, my entire body vanish.
Without even a heartbeat to break the silence, I simply gaze down at the wet floor.
It says "disinfectant,"
But I heard nothing about *myself* disappearing.
Or, was that actually true?
What could possibly prove that a human being wasn't "poison"?
I had long been a gentle poison.
With an infinite sense of relief, I slept better that night than I had in a long while.

I opened the door to my apartment
And found the Me of one year ago.
My pale face peeked out
From the shadows of a tower of books.
"Who is it…?" For a brief moment, we stared at each other, then the Me of one
year ago broke the ice.
"Is it still the year 2020?"
"It's 2021. July 23."
"That's great! So that thirtieth birthday just passed, eh?"
"I think we have more important things to discuss here."
"What happened this past year?"
To Tokyo? To me / you? Where should I even begin? I adjust my sweat-moistened,
non-woven mask. You *stay-homed* obsessively and vaccines came out, but maybe
you already knew that? Did you get your booster? As my questions rolled out, she
stared expressionlessly at a single spot on the floor. "You may be getting killed," she
suddenly tells me.

Killed? By who?   I don't know, but just existing is poison, so if you don't stay home you'll be killed. Right, but here I am living. Can you call this lifestyle *living*? Yes yes, you are indeed living, congratulations. My kidding didn't seem to resonate with her, and she abruptly shouts, *Shut up!*, crouches down hugging her knees. This is too much, I want to die, kill me, she is ranting. What an annoying woman. And to think *this* is the other me.

It was supposed to be gone.
It is not gone.
Dying at home. Dies with no company, no visitors.
Pushed down because she is a woman,
Stabbed to death because she "looked happy."
They are told to die alone.
Any inconvenient existence is deemed poison,
And relegated to a "parallel world."
Proceed. Kick aside your rigid body.
Reluctant to be taken away, even by myself,
I will not be killed without a fight.

Extend a hand, stomp a pedal, and disinfectant sprays out. The sound emanating from the thermometer makes people faintly nervous. The disinfectant placed around the city supposedly eliminates not only viruses, but also entire human beings which it considers poison.
However, complete elimination is impossible. So there is a quarantine apparatus to hide it from sight. As though by locking it away, you can no longer see inside, like those transparent "courtesy" toilets around Tokyo.

In front of Shibuya Station at dusk, a large truck drives by with a sign: "A state of emergency has been declared. Let's make this summer the last one spent at home!" A man's voice echoes on vacantly, "People of Tokyo, we appreciate your cooperation." The Me of one year ago ignores it blissfully, gleefully going about her life, as we make our way up Dogenzaka. The TOKYO 2020 logo pops out at even intervals.

Another state of emergency declared? So the Olympics must be canceled too, right? Is Tokyo right in the head? I hold Me's hand as she continues asking.
No one is sane.
Because to remain sane
It is insanity itself.
"Let me show you."

We start running without the Olympic torch and
To the passersby who turn to look and see what we're doing, we yell,
"We're infected!" and the streets immediately open up.

It's spreading!
It's spreading!
It's spreading!

Die alone!
Don't drag me into your contagion!
Bathed in spectatorless applause,
I pull Me's hand tighter,
Making our way toward
The red fireworks erupt over the Opening Ceremony
In the new National Stadium.
I will not leave you alone.
I will not let anyone disappear.
If you you think people can just vanish,
I dare you to try erasing them!
I race right into the transparent public bathroom
And without hesitation give that disinfectant pedal a mighty stomp.

Memorandum to Future Readers:

Commentators say Kawasaki attacker "Should have died alone!" provoking fears of inciting suicide, further incidents —*Mainichi Shimbun Digital*, May 31, 2019.

Tokyo Olympics, Paralympics to be postponed "About one year," will retain "Tokyo 2020" branding —BBC News, March 24, 2020.

Tokyo Governor Koike declares "Tokyo Alert," Rainbow Bridge and Tokyo Metropolitan Government building lit up in red —ANN News, June 2, 2020.

A public restroom with see-through walls opens in Shibuya!? When locked, the walls become opaque: We asked if there won't be any malfunctions —FNN Prime Online, August 6, 2020.

"Vaccination is hospitality," quips Hashimoto Seiko, Organizing Committee for the Olympics —*Mainichi Shimbun*, June 9, 2021.

Tokyo Metropolitan Government declares state of emergency for the fourth time, all of which were during the Olympics —NHK, July 9, 2021.

Tokyo Olympics Opening Ceremony begins. Postponement, no spectators —one anomaly after another —*Mainichi Shimbun*, July 23, 2021.

I turned 30 years old on July 23.
Fuzuki Yumi @luna_yumi —Twitter, July 24, 2021.

As covid cases peak, Tokyo Governor Koike Yuriko: "Especially for those who live alone, their homes should be their primary care center" —*Tokyo Shimbun*, July 28, 2021.

New coronavirus cases: Tokyo homecare cases rise five times more than prior month; over 10,000 cases nationwide —NHK, July 28, 2021.

IOC PR chief: "The Olympics is a parallel world. The outbreak did not spread from us." Meanwhile, the number of coronavirus infections climbs to the largest ever — *Tokyo Shimbun*, July 29, 2022.

Tokyo and the Olympics are "like parallel worlds." Record 3,865 people infected with coronavirus in Tokyo, but IOC denies connection —*Chunichi Sports*, July 29, 2021.

10 people seriously injured on Odakyu train, 36-year-old man arrested for attempted murder: "I just thought I'd like to kill a happy-looking woman," pours vegetable oil on the floor —*Tokyo Shimbun*, August 7, 2021.

84 people infected with coronavirus died at home in the past six months —NHK, August 3, 2021.

Number of coronavirus deaths while recuperating at home, Ministry of Health, Labor and Welfare says, "We don't know" —*Asahi Shimbun*, August 10, 2021.

49-year-old man arrested for obstructing business by shouting "I have corona!" —*Asahi Shimbun Digital* March 26, 2020.

MORIYAMA MEGUMI

tr. Yasuhiro Yotsumoto, Michele Hutchison, & Moriyama Megumi

Mid-Air

Dangle
by the fragile ankles, not
having been able to find Yourcenar's perfect shoes*
                                    to fit my feet, and

I, who
wanted to get everywhere on my own but couldn't,
suffer, with the falling ashes,

                                    a crash.

Sucked into a flow-
er, er, er……, the faint sound of it,   and an ant following it, all of us

            falling, falling,
                        and going, going,   deep down.

Where have the bodies of those women gone, who
                        jumped from the cliff, after the war,
                                    one after another…?

You see,
even after a hundred or a thousand years,
                        they have still reached nowhere.*

Their voices have been incessantly denied,
                        suspended, in
            mid-air.

Fight, fight!   Virginia spurred herself on.*

The voices, which have been crushed each and every time,
swelling back again and again....

    "As a flake that the wind whirls skywards from the snow-drift on the frozen
    shore   hangs in the air and vanishes, so shall I end my days."*

Ukifune, the last princess in the Tale of Genji, was going to hang herself in
               mid-air,   yet, with her own will,
             with her fragile ankles,   took a calm footstep

forward into the whirling water.
Like her own name, Floating Boat, her life was full of misery, but
no matter how many times erased, her voice, though quivering,
persists in her poetry.

Ah, Women,
Ye shall not let yourselves die.*
I cry over you,
Ye shall not ever let yourselves be silenced.

       The tongue having been squeezed down to the bottom of a flower,
     now curling and crawling out
   through the narrow throat,   oozing out.

The red-soled-stiletto Louboutins never fit my feet, were never really craved,
nor their lukewarm consolation.

       kicking the heel, I take a plunge
into mid-air.

---

*Quotations from: Yourcenar's Shoes (ユルスナールの靴) by Suga Atsuko
      "Cliff" (崖) by Ishigaki Rin
      The Waves by Virginia Woolf
      "Ukifune" (浮舟) chapter from *The Tale of Genji* (源氏物語)
      "Don't you dare die" (君死にたまふことなかれ) by Yosano Akiko

SELECTED POEMS FROM *KŪKI NO NIKKI* (AIR DIARIES) 2020–2021

MATSUDA TOMOHARU
tr. Julia Hansell Clark

Wednesday, April 1, 2020

toilet paper was stolen from the paper recycling
in front of the entranceway
on the third day after shimura ken died
i watched the tribute show and laughed
what will happen next
they say the public high school's new semester is postponed another
month
the children not in school don't even change their clothes
the voices saying don't be a perpetrator grow loud
the city governor says, don't go to bars at night
says, don't go to karaoke or live shows
doesn't it sound like a death sentence to those involved

the fatality of the novel coronavirus is said to be 2-3%
this hasn't changed since the chaos first started
the variant is us
the 2-3% in the distance
and the 2-3% right beside us
are so very different

this year the cherry blossoms bloom early
and strangely fail to scatter

2 masks each passed out to every household
the masked prime minister announced

Setagaya, Tokyo

KAWAGUCHI HARUMI
tr. Matias Chiappe Ippolito

Saturday, April 18, 2020

Unbearably flowing and spilling from the thin sky
cherry blossoms that bloomed hurriedly like premonitions
as the sky was lightened up
and then snow, as if rushing to cover them,
falling and piling up, a weekend three weeks ago
that time
in which April had not arrived yet
and even though I had given up on Aprils
I did my best to take my softest pencil
and since then
draw lines every day
each item written in my favorite notebook
crossed, one after the other
I kept crossing them out
appointments meetings arrangements encounters
canceled postponed called-off abandoned
for an illusionary
semi-transparent membrane wrapped them
and gently isolated them more and more
every time I passed the pages the strikethroughs of resignation
stretching over the worn-out days
softly selling up
chick's wet feathers or buds of ruin
so it goes nothing can be done we'll meet some other time
we'll survive and meet
and so we live
are
but
what was supposed to be my plan is gone too soon
I myself am turning thinner and lighter

where the hell am I?
taken away by the blackened fluffy strikethroughs
of a vanished April
I may be nowhere to be found, but
I wash and wash and wash my hands
I put on my mask
today, the rain
like dotted lines made to separate
poured down innumerable strikethroughs
and yet, the sound of the rainfall reaches
the edges my ears right here
in this night of rising rain
I listen to En Hosaki and Hirata Yū reading my poems
several years ago, via TwitCasting
the words I remember surge with different voices
then go back inside of me
and I welcome them
I cry a little
I open myself that bottle of sparkling wine I had bought in March thinking I would
drink it with a friend
bubbles of fleeting light
popping up like buds like beads of words I don't know
mingling together and pouring down again
inside of me.

Jingumae, Tokyo

---

* "a weekend three weeks ago": it snowed in Tokyo on Sunday, March 29th, the day
that comedian Shimura Ken passed away from coronavirus-induced pneumonia.

JORDAN A. Y. SMITH

Monday, May 4, 2020

Through the Dokodemo Zoom Window
Stay-at-home carnage
        Domestic circus
                        zoomed-in on another desert island
In digital backgrounds
    Pieces erasing the senses of places
        in chessboardrooms
I'm unraveling
                – *fine* –
        I'm Time/
                    traveling

Last year's *kigo*:
        natsu-no hada – summertime skin
            muda-ge – needless hair
                kirei – beautiful, rendered in katakana
                    wakiase taisaku – anti-armpit sweat tactics

This year's *kigo*:
        (None. Train ad spaces lie fallow.)

俳句 haiku、零時 reiji、0:00 is time for h i c r a z y

ラン乱イ ラン欄違乱いらん、蘭
    LAN war, Iran land riot not needed, orchids
        選船千線専戦せんといて
        choice ships thousand stripes specialty fights, don't do it
            チョー長朝町長蝶々よ、超
            super long matins town mayors butterflies, hyper
                孝行高校や航行煌煌
                filial piety high school or dazzling cruise
                    1湾1ワンワン1腕,、no one won、no王
                        1 bay 1 dog 1 arm no one won no king no one wonders when done

Must free
The ear and ear
Shackled to headphones
Or the gradually escalating noise,
Which may be sirens, or remnants of a day nearly gone quiet
Will become indistinguishable.

On those fragments above falls a light drizzle of hope
Traces the digressing line of medical care, pharmaceuticals,
And you don't say,
One day on Mercury
Is 58.6 days for us on Earth…

Kagurazaka, Tokyo

MIYAO SETSUKO

tr. Matias Chiappe Ippolito

Sunday, May 10, 2020

"That's what you do."
If I had to put it in words, that would be it.
An office worker whose wife was a nurse
was told by his boss:
"You either take holiday leave or your wife quits."
The Pandemic Police had reached town.
Cars with plates from other prefectures were scratched.
Stores not entering into voluntary restraint (not following
the official self-restraint regulations) had stones thrown at them.
After the nationwide declaration of a State of Emergency
(such things happen)
an abnormal phenomenon is emerging among the people
(such things happen).
"Neighbors are the scariest,"
were the words of a man during wartime.
"Self-righteousness is scarier than the sourness of summer oranges,"
are the words I utter today.
And something else.
The hashtag *IAmAgainstThePublicProsecutorOfficeLaw*
spreads like flames on Twitter
and quickly starts trending
(I am protesting, not opposing… better I guess).
But then, a bizarre phenomenon. From around
2 million tweets,
the number of posts in front of my eyes started decreasing
in a rush, as the moon waning.
"That's what you do."
"No one told me to do that."
(It's always this…).
Though the moon wanes (I'll tell you what),
the Heavens are watching.

Hanno, Saitama

ARAI TAKAKO
tr. Jeffrey Angles

Sunday, June 7, 2020

Go somewhere as quiet as possible
And try whispering the word
Tamashii, meaning "spirit"

The tip of your tongue strikes the palette with the *ta*
Your lips, tied together, separate with the *ma*
By the time you've said *tama* (soul)
The sound of the drum inside your mouth
Begins to fall, doesn't it,
Through the deep well of your throat
Forming a *ma* (space)
Somewhere deep inside the body

Tama, tama, tama
The more you repeat it, the more the echoes collect in the swamp of your stomach
Do you remember? Once there were those who thought of such things
As *ma* (enchantment)

Now,
Try speaking softly
As you add the *tama* (soul)
To the *shii* leaking from the space between your teeth

Tama, tamashii—soul, spirit
Tama, tamashii—soul, spirit
This time the enchantment is lifted from the swamp
Wrapped in white breath
It rises
Its tail leaking a trail
Of smoke from the mouth

Tamashii—the spirit
Is a thing that moves
Something that will continue to move

"I can't breathe"

Even in the last moments of life
It is a moving thing
Something that moves and spreads out wide

Yokohama, Kanagawa

MATSUDA TOMOHARU
tr. Julia Hansell Clark

Tuesday, June 9, 2020

the red government building's warning that the problem has moved from the virus
    to the people
seems an omen of a rift that will only grow from here
more than a catastrophe, these conditions that no one can lift
are like a strange season that comes once in a hundred years

mosquitoes sting
even in light clothes
not a single child is sunburned
masks are overflowing in the streets
although we're all only talking to machines

Setagaya, Tokyo

Thursday, July 16, 2020

contagion surges in a wave
the catastrophe is endless, so
from here cities will decay and
village building will begin, i imagine
we will split japan into 20000 villages and
rebuild from scratch
if there are shrines
then we will have to choose religions, so we hold off
and call them interim shrines
interim priests at interim shrines
will say interim prayers for us
the interim mayor and interim parliament members will talk at the interim assembly
and make interim rules
but even before that
first we need villagers
doctors
dentists
farmers
ranchers
hunters
fishers
grocers
butchers
fish stores
rice stores
potters
foresters
woodworkers
carpenters
tile workers

lacquer workers
metalsmiths
lathe operators
press operators
weavers
dyers
printers
paper sellers
paper folders
book binders
bakeries
candy stores
liquor stores
leather stores
purse stores
bike stores
sign stores
umbrella stores
shoe stores
clothing stores
kimono stores
zōri stores
geta stores
construction workers
demolition workers
building contractors
masons
concrete mixers
waste treatment workers
welders
machinists
glass stores
mirror stores
painters
furniture stores
music stores
stationary stores
book stores
gardeners

chiropractors
masseuses
fortune tellers
accountants
toy stores
cake stores
audio stores
frame stores
framers
hardware stores
variety stores
dried good stores
tea stores
oden stores
izakaya
bars
cafes
takoyaki stands
monja stands
okonomiyaki stands
web designers
liquor stores
breweries
soy sauce stores
publishers
local papers
journalists
fishing tackle stores
model kit stores
musicians
architects
designers
artists
theater troupes
singers
piano classes
bands
instrument shops
calligraphers

abacus schools
cram schools
sports shops
golf shops
used bookstores
antique stores
record stores
florists
appliance stores
car dealerships
snack bars
brothels
banks
markets
schools
police
firemen
inns
hotels
movie theaters
bathhouses
funeral homes
cleaners
novelists
photographers
flower arrangers
tea ceremony practitioners
comedians
dancers
dance classes
poets
tanka poets
haiku poets
crossing guards
we will have everyone gather
and make the very best village
we can't cover every trade so each village will specialize and divide labor
to what extent can jobs be reduced to the essentials
i recall a tsutsui yasutaka novel where sounds disappear one by one
between villages cars like balloons will come and go

during epidemics traffic will be stopped
people will interact digitally, with friends around the world
and companies unbound by place will connect to do big work
but special things will gradually become unnecessary
everyone will travel to see festivals in beautiful villages
fall in love there, and change their residence
good people will move to villages with good reputations
and villages without will have villagers rely on digital content
and grow empty
a disparity in wealth will form
what is the minimum necessary infrastructure
we'll surely need to deal with the graves

raindrops flew into the *obon* bonfire and made a concrete sound
the smell of ash spread

tokyo was cut out from the campaign

Setagaya, Tokyo

ARAI TAKAKO
tr. Kendall Heitzman
Thursday, July 23, 2020

I turned over the leaf
without any design in mind
when one found me:
ranks of reddish-brown spots, a precise pattern,
and not just here—
on this one, on this one, on this one as well.

Once, when I was four,
I was put to bed early, feverish.
When I awoke, I stood in front of my mother's vanity
to find horrible spots
on my face, on my neck, on my arms and legs as well.
I got into her lipstick, and smeared it across my face.

I cried, I cried, oh, how I cried,
but those unbearable spots wouldn't go away.

What is this fear?
What is this fear of infection?
I ask now,
and that scene comes back to me,
the motley pattern printed on my heart.

We can actually see it, can't we?
The virus,
those reddish-brown spots,
the exact moment it came breezing in.

It's because . . .
we can see it . . .
that it's terrifying.

I cry, I cry, oh, how I cry,
but they don't disappear from

my face, my neck, my arms and legs.

Yokohama, Kanagawa

YOTSUMOTO YASUHIRO
tr. Matias Chiappe Ippolito

Monday, January 4, 2021

It seems the prefectural governors have asked
the central government to consider the Declaration.
It seems the central government will take into account
the opinion of experts.
Meanwhile, the central government urged
the prefectural governors to move forward with the measures
and the latter said they would comply with the request.
Welcome to the Wonderland that is Japan.
Who is asking who
and what are they asking?
Who is requesting and who is complying
and whom of those is deciding and why isn't it a Declaration
but a "Consideration" of a Declaration?
And what on earth is an unenforceable Declaration anyway?
Is it something like the
Humanity Declaration?
Or is it closer to the Spring Traffic Safety Declaration?
Anyhow, they are all the same in that they are not "Laws,"
there's no way to reject them or approve them
instead of enforcing them.
Like a song, these are but words recited to the sky.
Under unspoken petals that dance down
fluttering and thrilled
a man and a woman
wrapped by the anonymity of their ceremonial kimonos
hug each other
as if there was no room for
even a single particle of the virus to creep in
they lie down, skin tightly over skin.
Their rib cages creak.
The woman buries her face on the man's chest.
My hair stands on ends just of imagining

that the one being embraced ecstatically is a governor
and the one chuckling faintly while facing up,
twitching his or her nose, is the central government.
Unexpectedly, one of them (both, depending on the case)
might even be you.
Knowing thyself is a hard thing. Even more so,
no one can open up their eyes widely and look upon their own sleeping face.
Everywhere a petal touches
crimson bruises will bloom on their soft skins.
On the *tokonoma*, death,
cold sweat forming,
as *kaki* fruits left unsold from last year.
Lust and corrosion mix together
an indescribable smell grows up like a fetus, but
though I open the *shōji*, the windows cannot be opened.

Yokohama, Kuboyama

ENOMOTO SACLACO

tr. Eric Selland

Poème Symphonique for 100 fragments

(Un texte en hommage à György Ligeti)

00

What is placed there before us is a still life… or not.

01

No need for concerns about immorality. What is standing before us is not a gigantic Trojan horse, but one reed, so to speak.

02

Grape vines cling to the wings of the silver-plated fetus of a mythical beast that devours dreams, but the delicate ankles of the merciful shepherd have bloody teeth marks.

03

Who painted the taxidermy of a certain marriage with coal tar?

04

Multiple ears grow from the rigid rat corpse in the dark green perfume bottle, but it doesn't mean as much as a molten bronze neck.

05

A screw is fitted to a twilight Mars and above the dangling chromosomes the celestial globe blinks, then under the feeble light of a fluorescent lamp cut through by the afterimage of a girl who ought to have grown on an apple tree, the screams of leather shoes can be heard.

06

On an evening of driving wedges into a number of inconspicuous constellations and waiting for the brandy to be poured, frost alights on the lens of the monocle.

07

The quietly trembling tail of the rainbow-colored lizard that creeps along the cell wall penetrates the orbit of a wildcat and drowns in the bright urine of a pregnant woman.

08

The oval shape of something dry and murky whose name I don't know licks the morning dew which slides gently along the blade of the cutting shears.

09

The lid of a vessel— perhaps being randomly placed on the sand is the destiny of salt flame.

10

Was Pegasus born so that he could be heated by the bell of a clock tower?

11

Once again segments of mica dance before a number of fingers.

12

The counterfeit window reflecting the shadow of the zelkova tree rusted white and the mold in the cage glowing faintly become increasingly smoky while creating a whirlwind, and the right arm of the plaster statue along with the melted ice nods toward the east on the edge of the glass.

13

Bound tightly with unknown characters, an ant drifts along the rough skin.

14

Going around the inside of the water pipe awakening headless scales, then crouching in the raw cotton without getting wet in the rain.

15

Crushed hands, the fingernails of the one grasping at my throat, blind gymnosperms and a faded letter on a dust-covered table, this too is a lie.

16

Remembering the delay of the cicada, even if you take the candles out of the ears upside-down, nothing falls out.

17
A rhinoceros* visits a crumbling brick house that no one will go near, while the
sweet flesh of the mango drooling on its back tries to break the smooth outline of a
mannequin, burning to death the ancient squid embedded in the cold wall.

18
On the fertile plain of monkeys, the conflict with metal soap did not turn into a riot.
The only disappointing thing was that a few goldfish ate the remaining bubbles.

19
No matter how much the doorbell rings, leaking light ink from the side of the
mouth, which net should one use to capture the wheezing that cannot be heard
through that hole called a vent or aperture?

20
Stuff a new cow horn into your bag and hold it up to Wednesday's sunlight— any
oil will do.

21
Spend each day tied to a stick, struck by golden ears of wheat, drinking a deaf-mute
with a vase over his head, afraid of the cries of unknown birds.

22
Go to a forest of copper overgrown with moss inflating drops of water on a
dangling holiday.

23
Most of the structures are indistinguishable from a lake overflowing with memory
that makes one think of balloons. In that sense, neither color nor fragrance is
enough to spoil the roots of medicinal herbs.

24
The dream of the book appears in the midst of a busy coma, like looking into the
compound eye of a bee.

25
Why on earth would someone erect a cross which has lost its symbolism on top of
a cliff, shouts the eagle.

26

Seven pianos, a television on the altar hiding the figure of Vishnu, a lemon and forceps stretched out, and a table with nothing to do but wait for it to be peeled.

27

The distress of developing a fever, making one's way through the darkness of the spindle-shaped thicket, where eventually the hardened entrails of the dried reeds develop cracks.

28

Held in bondage by the ghost of an air gun, hating the gills pulling up the fishing bucket, the castle of chalk revived by growth rings kisses the decayed steel, and invites a skin rash to come before the kneeling brush.

29

A region of dairy farms sporting goatees, a puppet's arm crosses the sea of diluted juice, only to be run over and killed by some sticky beeswax, while the fiddler traverses the branches of Japanese larch.

30

Wishing for the bloated formula of a bear crouching behind a mirror.

31

Following the broken strings of sleep, the first spider licks the saturated obituaries of stars, and in that universe, a giant fishing rod is carefully lowered into the beak of a young pigeon.

32

There's just no way the false story can end without offering the neck the hand will strangle to the wet nurse strumming a lute with frozen electromagnetic waves.

33

A radiant folding screen with a painting in which a spleen and a volcano are devouring light-red flowers of water lilies blooming in the bathtub.

34

A flock of weekly magazines has domesticated the heat haze residing in empty marmalade bottles.

35
They burned magnesium to guide the carbonized crucifixion back to the fusion
reactor by roasting multiple illusions entwined in the steel cord wire.

36
To imprison the cryptograph that rises in the middle of the tranquil garden, have a
remote low-pressure system hit it from both sides.

37
Then they dragged out a prime number of ankles from the northern region which
had remained concealed, crushed obsidian causing the morning to stagnate on the
tips of their toes.

38
Wind crests, sinking an accordion to the bottom of a dry lakebed, on a desk where
petals bend softly.

39
In the midst of reminiscing over a letter, the ghost of snow or sleet bites off the
breasts, leaving only the burnt eyes of a duck to weep.

40
A headache that, with no one around, only the sound of the footsteps of an
inebriated panther can respond to, the frozen aborted waterfall, the easy chair that
looks like a bad fit, like a butterfly loving a walnut shell.

41
A tumor that will destroy the camellias and cause the drowning of sea beasts.

42
All extinctions are inserted into the brutal cheek pouch of this troublesome
afternoon, and the moistened silence flirts with the abrasions.

43
Hearing the painter's raindrops struck by the heat of the withered grass, the
bleeding voice does not interfere with nostalgia in the least.

44

The lustrous haze covering the sighs of the sleeping sharks inverted by the lunar
eclipse in the twilight of evening is pale with righteous indignation at the mirage
that keeps blinking off and on.

45

I search for the traces beyond the soda water, the love of the golden sparrow, the
fire on the rocky shore where the mollusk's tongue is wagging, and the cobalt's
despair depicted in the triangular flag.

46

In the flooded archive where records are spinning, aquatic insects with their wings
torn off communicate by rubbing their exoskeletons.

47

The acrylic lies squeezed in between the folds of a greeting are surrounded by
smoke exhaled by a fox and become necrotic.

48

The sandstorm-infested pine lamps flash whale oil and pour their iridescence on the
poisoned ginseng tucked away in the rib cage.

49

The figure of a horse with rolled-up eyelids is engraved on the underside of a
bronze wheel.

50

It's not a bile curse or anything like that, just a record of how the invaded mercury
crystals eventually disintegrated.

---

* the word for rhinoceros in Japanese (*sai*) also means "when" or "upon".
Hearing this sentence, the listener would assume that it means: "when visiting a
crumbling brick house."

TAKAHASHI MUTSUO
translated by Jeffrey Angles

Selections from *Only Yesterday*

Older Sisters, Younger Brother
> *Electra, Orestes, Iphigeneia*

Sister makes a bold resolve, brother stays indecisive—isn't that always the way?
The day of father's departure, one sister weeps as younger brother romps
When mother has her affair, sister watches while brother sleeps like a log
As mother murders father, soon after his triumphant return,
Sister listens to the screams, hiding in the maiden's chambers
Driven by a distant relative, brother runs with dog through fields and mountains,
Knowing nothing, he returns, sister rushes to him, clamoring for revenge
Full of fear, brother kills mother—sister dances for joy, shouts with delight
But when matricidal regret drives him mad, the instigator is nowhere to be found
It is the other sister who must purify the mad wanderer, she who should have been
The living sacrifice as father waited to set sail—suddenly she appears,
Great goddess from the machine—without her, he could not live—
But so what if he did not? In any case, it is without a doubt his sister
Standing up straight on the midday stage, full of ferocity and kindness too

Agave Speaks to Pentheus
The Bacchae

You're my son, you say? Who do you mean? I've got no clue
I don't remember giving birth, nor raising any child like you
Behold my breasts, still fresh, pointed, and virginal!
Only the flushed lips of young gods have drunk from them—
I'd rather give them to suckling pigs than share with anyone else
Mother, you say? Remember, you beg? Oh, hairy beast—
You were not born of my belly, unblemished by scar or spot,
I brim with the energy of a virgin, yet undefiled
I'll rip you apart—hands, legs, head—and toss you away
Your dismembered hands will be nothing more than hands,
Your legs nothing more than legs, your head a mere head
May each part weep its own tears, scream its own screams!
Meanwhile, I'll paint both breasts with the blood staining my fingers
And to coat my belly, I'll lick up any blood that remains
That will be your funeral—may you accept it gratefully!

Hatred of Heroes

Speaking out against Alexander

I hate heroes—the reason is that heroes do not love us
If we do not obey their wishes, our cities and people burn
The fact he left a poet's house standing unscorched
Doesn't make up for his actions, if the poet was alive
I cannot imagine he'd have gone along so willingly
The poet and his home would have been torched in the end
Some say if there were no heroes, the world wouldn't end
It's unbearable that people must die for the world to change
Who needs change anyway? The world and I can stay just as we are
Changing by its very nature means approaching some end
If heroes want change so much, they should concentrate
On their own worlds, let them do with them as they like
Let them retreat into their own worlds and leave us the hell alone

After a Siesta

Forceful, strong sleepiness rules the afternoon hours but
It's not just people who fall sound asleep, dead to the world
The streets, trees, shadows, and the cloudless blue sky above
All stare through open windows into the darkness inside—
An unlucky, young god in profile with winged shoes and winged staff—
Then at long last, the fulfilled sleepers get up and slowly go outside,
Stepping into the cool breeze and sunlight, never quite realizing
The time spent asleep has brought them that much closer to death

The Poet and the Blind Man

Backtracking through the paper trail like an archaeologist
It appears that the original Homer was not necessarily blind—
You spoke with such abandon to the sparse group of listeners
Gathered there in the cool shade of the hill above the port
Tenedos is the island where the fabled Achaean forces hid their fleet,
Pretending to be in retreat. So why many generations later,
Is it necessary for us to pretend the poet was blind?
Because with our spit, we listeners swallow down our bubbling doubts,
Gaze up at the sun filtered through the treetops, and think,
This is a problem we must ponder over time
The next morning, we faced Troy and recited The Iliad as the sun rose
The Greeks in Greek, the Turks in Turkish, the Germans in German,
And as I recited in Japanese, I kept closing my eyes over and over
Just like the kindness of the heroes to the elderly, enemy king
The sunlight blinded me overhead

Beautiful Grave

The world's most beautiful grave must be the oar erected to shipwrecked sailors
Beneath the upside-down oar, no corpses are there
Cast to the waves, they dissolved and now lap unknown shores
Ultimately, all humans are shipwrecked on society's salty seas
Slowly forgotten until gone from memory—how appropriate then
That the marker is of wood that will rot, not immutable stone
But more beautiful yet would have been a grave with no marker at all
The back-and-forth swell of the sea would serve as burial mound
With no marker other than an occasional rainbow overhead

Fragments

In its cruelty, history smashed poetry to smithereens
But that was not always an entirely negative thing
Fragments that barely survived only as quotes
Become the spirits of poems once complete
The light they emit entices future generations
And from them, new poems begin—the life force of poetry
Lies in the ability to constantly birth new beginnings

To the Artists

More than the artists who left behind sculptures
Of gods, goddess, young men, and maidens
It was the artists who entrusted all their creations
To loss who managed to achieve true beauty
Beauty in this world is makeshift and transitory
Gaze upon the true beauty that lies beyond!—
Even the words of the wise men who repeat such things
Are stones that trip us up on the way to truth
What good is it, you ask, if we feel the lust swell
At the sculptures' broad chests or glistening thighs?
Oh, artists of Greece! It is because your works
Disappeared so completely without a trace
That I sing your praises now, and once I am done,
May these words of praise also fade to oblivion

Ultimate Wisdom

Isn't this the ultimate wisdom—
That all good things come from others
And all bad things come from the self?
What's more, when one thinks this way
If nothing but bad should come
One should be deeply grateful and
Thank the unknown gods because
Hardships sharpen you like a knife,
Polishing your surfaces that much more
Grind, sharpen, polish—if in all of this
You find yourself worn away to nothingness
That's where you will find joy, for there
Nothing will be left to cause you pain
Because you will exist everywhere
And nowhere at the same time

Readying a Needle

"Always have a sewing needle ready in your change purse"
This is the precious wisdom shared by generations of grandmothers
If you trip and fall somewhere on your path, stick the needle
In the spot you struck before picking up your walking stick again
It's important to let a little blood flow, to expose it to the air
Blood goes bad when it gets engorged, endangering life itself
That's why old folks who fall just lie there and die without getting up
All you need to stop someone from losing consciousness and passing away
Is a single needle—a pretty cheap solution if you ask me
What's more, when you can no longer bear to behold your own sins
You can poke out your eyes and convert the world to darkness

Giacometti's Walking Man

Like an Egyptian statue, the kouros faces forward,
Expressionless and stiff. One day his cheeks grow thick
And lift his tightly pursed lips into the faintest smile
His arms hang, palms pressed flat against his thighs,
As his left leg slides slightly forward, then his right
He steps forward, crouches down to throw a discus
For ages, he grips a club in a fighting pose, then sits in thought,
Chin balanced on his hand. After long contemplation,
He cuts away all muscle, all expression, becoming little more
Than the lines of a walking man. Before long, he'll be
The merest trace of movement—the movement contained in
That earliest smile, that earliest step, so simple
And unsophisticated, twenty-six centuries before

ART BY
SHIRAISHI SETSUHI

Beauty 美 (2011)

Beauty 美 (2012)

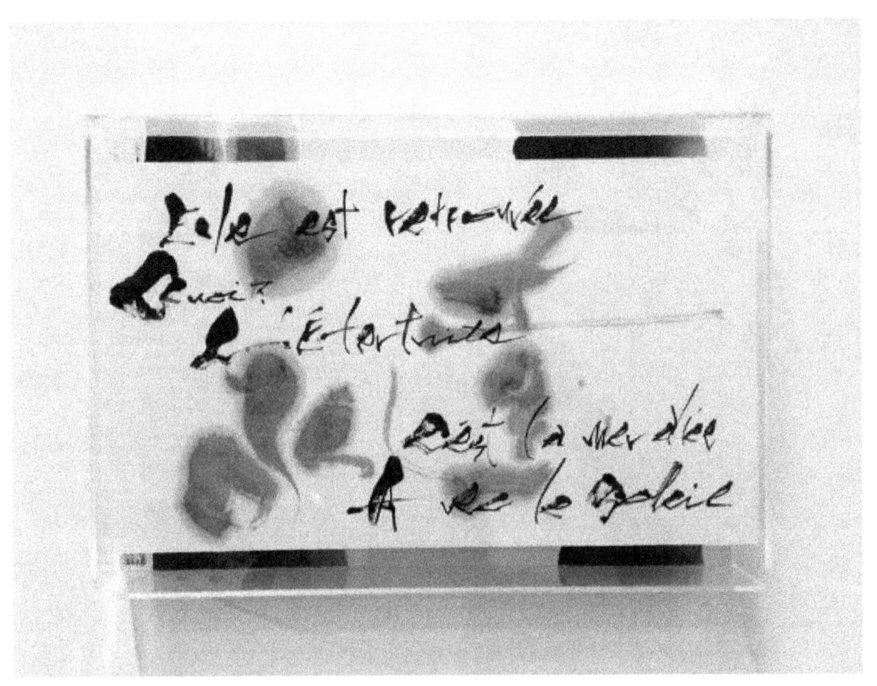

Eternity~Sun Paired with Sea 永遠〜太陽と番った海〜 (2014)

"Elle est retrouvée,
Quoi?—L'Éternité.
C'est la mer allée
Avec le soleil"

—Rimbaud

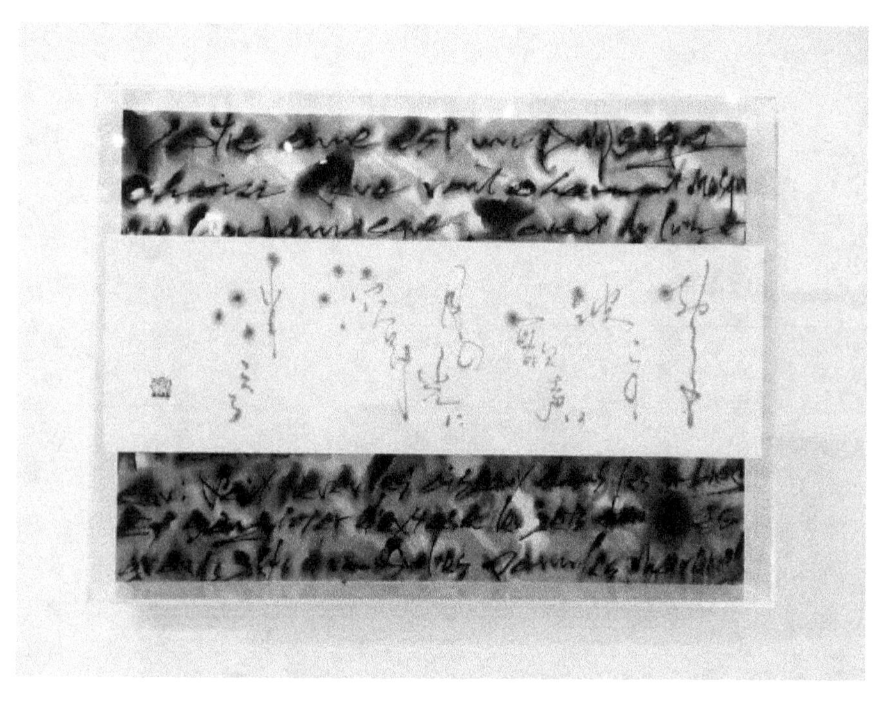

Moon and Sunlight 月の光 (2014)

Vicissitiudes of Perspective 視点の移ろい (2022)

One — (2022)

AOYAGI NATSUMI
tr. Jordan A. Y. Smith

Sea Goddess

In China during the Song Dynasty,
The size of the ocean
Was not so easy to imagine as it is today.
No one woke up early
To contemplate
Exotic towns.
The ocean existed only as barrier zone,
A place one couldn't set foot,
One stretching somewhere far away
To where the eye could not see.
If you had a ship,
You could float across.

Ship was born in the harbor.
Much time had passed since this Sea Goddess had come to be called Mazu.
Countless legends flew round about her,
She didn't cry when she was born, she was a blessing from Heaven, a child of high
    royalty,
The only thing truly known was that Ship often gazed at the sea with eyes that saw
    far into the distance.
Even the name Ship is one used here so we can speak of it,
though not a soul knows its true name.
But Ship was indeed an individual person.

One day, while Ship was gazing at the ocean, its eyes began to twitch,
And from its right eye popped a glass marble.
The sphere held the red of ocean twilight,
If held high it showed the sky as viewed from the ocean, if held low it showed the
    ocean floor.
Ship placed this tiny ocean in a bag and carried it everywhere.

The marble showed an ocean far away, with the time of day was slightly ahead,
So if it revealed a turbulent red ocean, Ship would advise everyone not to put out to
    sea that evening.

Ship's eye again began to twitch, and from the left eye, out popped another marble.
This one held the azure ocean of midday, and when Ship peered into this marble's
    blue,
Mary appeared, waiting far across the ocean.
Clouds crept across its sky,
And as the ashen sky stretched from morning through the day into night, the sea
    too grew ashen.
A tiny starlike light was seemingly gleaming,
But it was the candle Mary had lit on the far shore.
Inside the ashen marble, the flame flickered.
And in its light, Mary crafted her first tale.
The monster read books, listened to songs, learned that the first thing
to float in the sky was the Moon.
Mary gazed at the body the monster had been born with.
Ship gazed at Mary and the monster through the marble.

Then Ship peered into the marbles with both eyes, seeing as though
    inhabiting that world beyond,
And so contemplating, Ship came to forget that its own body was in fact right here.
And on that ocean which should have been impossible to enter, Ship set its body
    afloat.
At which moment Ship realized:
The ocean was not a divider,
When Ship touched one edge of the ocean, it was simultaneously touching some
    opposite edge.
And suddenly, the marbles became teardrops, teardrops became marbles,
    pouring from Ship's eyes,
A crimson rain, an azure rain, flowing down into the ocean.

Log

It was after the storm cleared.
A whale was stranded on the beach.
The whale gasped feebly,
In evident distress,
Right away, I phoned town hall.
They called in a specialist who began to treat it,
And from the whale's mouth
Removed a massive number of tablet computers.
One by one, they switched on the power,
And each booted up smoothly.
As each wifi reception kicked in,
Before long,
A distant sea appeared with ships bobbing here and there,
And as soon as they did,
Hundreds of ships appeared
Like a wall of buildings closing in.
Everyone climbed down from the ships,
began to pick up the tablets,
Saying, *Not this one, not that one either,*
As they checked the desktop background images,
Each looking for their own device.
Yes, every one
Of the tablets belonged to the sailors.
The moment they powered on,
The tablets the whale had swallowed
Began to transmit location information to the sailors' radar,
And glowed like bright stars.
The ship logbooks that remained
On the tablets the sailors left behind
Told of a giant woman they had encountered at sea.

The sailors swarmed back to their ships,
This time carrying something in their palms.
Each had a distinct form
And was dirty and damp.
Perhaps from being stored deep in the ship's hold.
The sailors again gathered together
Around the whale and placed the tiny forms around it.
The objects
Were ship spirits,
Guardian deities perched there,
Encircling the whale.
As they did,
Slowly the whale heaved itself forth,
All onlookers' hair stood on end,
And just like that the whale walked off.
The guardian deities
Watched over the figure as it left.

Landing

Something underground had been moving around.
It could make its way anywhere under the earth,

It found its way to the ocean floor.

Everytime it arrived somewhere,
A festival would break out.

Not a festival usually held in the area,
But one that spontaneously broke out upon the arrival.

In every region, it seemed as though people
Understood what was what.

They may also have been pretending to understand.

—

When something would pop its head up above ground,
It was at that exact spot the festival would occur.

Night after night, the townspeople pondered together what to do,
Perhaps the town's own festival and the festival of the something

Could be blended, they decided.
It was a monumental decision.

Children gathered at the town hall
To learn the dances.

The dances they learned there
Took traditional festival and spontaneous festival ways

And combined them.
They flapped their hands,
Waving their feet about in time,

Moving their bodies
Like fish or whales.

From the town to the ocean, stretching out like a breakwater,
A long thin line of portable wooden shrines,

On the opposite bank along the river stood
children who wove through the shrines

To form a circle, and they danced.

—

The furthest visible land was the mountain.
Round and round the children turned,

Circling the shrines, flapping hands and feet as they moved,
Then one by one

Each plucked a single hair
And blew them away in a puff of breath.

The thing underground

Followed the above ground festival, circling,
Climbing up the mountain,

Then turned into smoke and floated up to the sky.

The smoke drifted.

With neither wind nor navigator,

Mid-sky, being proclaimed suddenly free,
It found itself at a loss as to where to go.

The strands of hair from the children
Mounted the wind and took to the sky

And formed into a single baby dragon.

Together with the smoke, the dragon walked the sky,
Then found some new patch of earth, and dove deep down inside.

Butterfly

Her name is Ship.
Ship also had another name.
She also went by Wutip,
Or *Butterfly* in the language of Macau.

The name was born after Ship was born.
Wutip was a typhoon.
It was born in 2019 in the Marshall Islands.

The hestina assimilis is a type of butterfly from China.
With beautiful white spots over a black base,
and remarkable red stars on the backsides of its wings.

But come springtime, the red stars disappear,
And its wings turn a white base with gorgeous black line patterns.

There was a hestina assimilis butterfly.
This Chinese butterfly was released in Japan,
Then more were released en masse,
Some people wanted to transform into a Japanese butterfly.

The butterflies, knowing nothing of being brought somewhere,
To this unfamiliar land,
Knowing not if it were heaven or hell,
Born from eggs, then they flew to the sky,

Even if no one had prompted it,
They sought mates
And began to live together,

And before anyone had noticed,
In not more than a twenty year span,
They could be seen everywhere.

Without protective measures, the ecosystem faced collapse,
So the hestina assimilis was declared an invasive species,

So now even if you see them while you're out walking,
You're not allowed to catch them,
Even if they lay dying in the road,
Not allowed to save them.

Neither can you live with them,
But if you look around the town
They are hatching from eggs,
And emerging from their chrysalises, wings flapping.

Ship went by several names.
Once, back in 2019,
Wutip was born.

From that year on, as long as
Hestina assimilis was in Japan,
It was forbidden from interacting with people.

Typhoons have been named Wutip thrice before,
So the next with that name will be around 2025.

The typhoons that make the rounds of fourteen nations in Asia
Go by 140 names they cycle through each time one emerges.

That's why about every five to six years
They make the rounds until Wutip is born again.

Wutip traveled to the east of the Philippines,
Where it became a tropical cyclone.

RENA FUKAZAWA

tr. Melinda Smith & Rina Kikuchi

where the bodies are

They are working, the women, the ones who seem like elder sisters
working, so gracefully, to float something away
stilled things, stopped things, things which are no longer moving setting them,
     softly, gently,
placing them just so on the waves (careful, make sure they never fetch up anywhere)

The wet pleats of our skirts reflect the light, ash-grey,
they ripple, gently, invitingly, in the water
Underneath, moving between our legs,
the things, the beings, are jostling each other, muttering together,
resisting, uselessly,
as if scratching at the sky, just a bunch of corpses that have failed, even at dying
     (careful not to look them in the eye)

A woman, who seems like a mother, is singing, a semitone lower
In time with her song, the elder-sister ones
make their faces grin, un-grin, grin again, like leaves flipping in the wind (well done,
     well done, you're doing so well)
The mother-like one, who shriveled up long, long ago
sits forever atop the rock
refusing to give up mothering

They say that when tomorrow comes, I too
with my own hands, will be floating these off, these manbodies (gently, softly, don't
     let them break apart)
which one, I wonder, which of them is the one I should be pushing out and away?
In the far-off time before I became *we*
which is the body that sent mine under?
which one, which one

The stilled ones, the stopped fathers
we float them, send them off so gracefully (well done, well done, you're doing so
    well)
sunk to our waists in the soft, never-cooling blood of our mothers,
we work, trying to forget the men who stroked our hair, once upon a time, the size
    of their palms
again and again, time without number,
it seems, gracefully, beautifully, we will keep on shedding them, floating them away

start here

It all began right here.
I was a little over 20 years old
I had completely lost all my words
and so
by gathering bits and pieces from a pile of rubble
pulling them out, fitting them together
I made shapes from whatever came to hand.
At first it was really just a child's game
and as for what I made,
it was nothing, just the kinds of little things you could easily fit in the palm of your
    hand…but
while I was in the flow of it, making one after another,
I realised I could do more than just line them up in a row, I could layer them on top
    of each other
I went on, soon I got so I could build things that were bigger even than my own
    body
Gradually the number of sightseers began to grow
Among them, some appeared who kindly said they liked what I had made
Perhaps I, too, can build a tall tower, perfectly straight, I thought
At some point, looking up, looking only at the sky,
I forgot that the ground is a thing which can shake.

So, I lost the lot, again, but hey,
it's just that I've come back to the start.

FUKUDAPERO

In a Bugged Motel Room

盗聴されたラブホの部屋でしずかにすすんでいく百合の嘔吐

in a bugged motel room silently processed | a lily's puke

Mackerel Orbits

鯖の運行はわたしたちは朝を考案する
みどりの月日はあえないは
水兵線は手をふるは
下がりゆく地球

はたまり水にひたされる
時間を訪ねたがるカラ

（あなたの誕生日プレゼントどうしようか）

わたしたちの手
は露雨を追って修正されていく

波
滑
泪

しろく消えゆく航路の泡を
クジラの死骸だけが思っている

mackerel orbits   are   planning mornings
months and days
cannot meet
super marine hor*iz*on
wave your hands
dipping earths   are   soaked in still waters
try visit time

what should   with your
i do   birthday present

following snows and rains
hands must be corrected

water   skin
water   bone
water   eye

wake of a boat leaving   foam
a decomposing whale   imagines

Priest Mackerel

a left right hand clamps your throat
priests | passing | school of mackerel

左手と右の手であなたを扼殺する
坊さんたちが鯖のように通りすぎる

Space Mackerel

a float in space a mackerel's body split slashed ripped | knifely movement |

銀河に鯖
の身体の割って斬り裂く
ナイフの運動
の盲目は太陽ふたつ

it's blindness | plural suns

TŌMA HIROKO
tr. Victoria Young

For the Peacemakers

The season to face the history of this island has come around
The history of this island approaching 50 years since reversion

Reversion is not a cause for celebration but a turning point
from America to Japan
The bases still remain,
unexploded bombs are still being discovered
Post-war in perpetuity

A war that I did not experience,
the post-war history,
the irrationalities and contradictions,
can I properly hand it down?
The children,
as an adult I cannot allow their learning to end.

Now, on this same earth, another tragic war.
That this is happening today, in 2022, is hard to believe.
I want to cover my eyes from the cruel spectacle.

Those who know the love of God,
Those who live on an island that has known war.
We who are both,
as makers of peace,
must do the things that we can, one by one.

Translation

The hand that opens the next locker in the changing room
is adorned with a glittering watch
"Ai, that watch is *jōtō*"
Jōtō is clearly a compliment of the highest order
but their expression tells me that they are puzzled

"Hey, that watch is really cool"

My junior colleague tips the bottled beer into my glass
Tōtōtōtō
Before the words tumble out, I scramble to cram them down into my gut
The glass dyes yellow
"Ahh, that'll do"

"How can you be so *tehgeh*?"
"She's *fuyū*-ing again"
"What're you *turubattling* about?"

I want to speak with words that feel like home
but as the bemused faces of others float into view
I lose the ability to translate well.
I try and search for the right words in Japanese
But they don't radiate the colour of my island's words
Red to peach, yellow to nude, azure to water
The colours mute, something lacks

Unutterable words permeate my blood
Hurtling, swirling, curling through my veins
Until the airwaves connect me with a family who needs no translation
Until I raise a glass with my friends back home

In a corner of the factory
A careless head bumps into the machine
And lets out a small *agah*

YAMAZAKI SHŪHEI

tr. Kendall Heitzman

I just want to do something with you

A message just for you:
If I ever meet you, think of what we might do.
We could walk the streets all night until the dawn comes.
We could talk about so many meaningless things.

I know the day will come when I meet you,
you, whom I have never had the chance to meet.
The morning light of the city embraces the flowers,
and everything seems possible.
Right now, with you, I want:

To shoot a movie,
a nice, vacuous teen movie.
To put on a play,
a comedy would be nice, even if it's not that funny,
just something that in the end, makes amends.
Or maybe music?
We could start a rock band
playing the smallest known sounds in the world
without any instruments.

I just want to do something with you.
I just want to undo something with you.
If ever I meet you,
I want to laugh my fool head off with you,
at everything we will have left behind.

An umbrella in the smoldering autumn

An umbrella in the smoldering autumn
tells of a pair of beautiful birds.
We don't know their sex, or age, or where they are from.
It might be a sandy beach in a ramshackle fishing village
or the center of Ginza itself in Tokyo.
None of that matters anymore.
But you're getting ahead of yourself.

We talk about how,
now that the library of all that we knew
has been trampled flat,
the view has really opened up,
all the way to the horizon.
Now we can all bring our fruits to the table.
So abundant, so succulent,
they hardly seem to belong
to an age in which words carry so little meaning.

The signals are so elegant,
but still they regulate people
who yearn to be self-reliant.
When I was just a spent bottle
clattering down a slope,
a donkey who endured the darkest hours with you
told us a gentle story, laced with lies.
We cried
not because of the fabrications,
but because we wanted to love
all the creatures scuttling by
on the path between this place
and the next.

WAGO RYOICHI
tr. Ayako Takahashi & Judy Halebsky
Out of Range

December 21, 2015:

A man asks the person beside him,
Have you heard the policy?
"Decontamination efforts will not
extend to forests beyond the living range"

What does within the "living range" mean?
What does beyond the "living range" mean?
Wild boars and all sorts of other animals are moving
beyond their "living range"
into our "living range"
Are these animals in the "animal range"?

December 23, 2015:

Another man whispers,
"If the Takahama nuclear power plant is allowed to restart
it could generate fuel within a day"
"beyond the range of daily living" does not mean "decontaminated"
but does "within the living range" mean "restart"?

Another man interrupts,
"So, wild boars are under the jurisdiction of the Ministry of Health
domestic pigs are under the jurisdiction of the Ministry of Agriculture
what about the boar-pigs
when wild boars and pigs interbreed
which administration is in charge of that?

Another man asks about the possibility
of a ninth planet in our solar system
After that, they talk seriously and casually, sometimes arguing,
sometimes resting their hands on each other's shoulders

Soon they will call it a night and go back
to their own muteness out of range
A SHORT LIFE

If I were allowed to return home for just two hours
what would I do?

line up the shoes in the entryway
cry in the living room
pack my grandmother's picture
try to decide which books to take with me and then give up
see if the computer turns on

stare at my reflection in the bathroom mirror
sweating and sorrowing
try to fill the tub
check if the toilet will flush
open the refrigerator
see what things in there have been kept cold

the phone   with a dial tone
think about calling my Mom and Dad

in the bedroom   lie on the futon
close my eyes   breathe radiation

wind
the crash of waves
out the window   light between clouds
everyday life

  two hours gone

Post-Fukushima Interview #6

1.

a museum curator,
a Jomon era scholar
and also a Shinto priest

his family home is near the ocean
in the hours directly after the earthquake
he sheltered at the museum
in the mountains of Aizuwakamatsu
the people there, during a civil war,
fled for their lives

so many times, he made the long trip back
thinking about
home and the ocean

surprised to see the beach drained
as though it were hundreds of years ago
in a flash, he said, *the reclaimed coastline
changed into un-reclaimed land*

how should we live after the tsunami?
attend funerals?
mourn the dead?
talk to others standing in evacuation lines?

he goes back and forth to work
from the Jomon period
to this catastrophe

2.

seeing the damage, there's an awakening, a consciousness
something like an internal implosion

cherry blossoms open in a sudden flicker
waves crash
a voice echoes through the valley
a hunter's horn rings in the forest
a tall mast in the blue sea
and so, you start to think

me?
am I awake?
this world bursting from one starting place
everyone
everything at a boiling point?
am I a participant,
party to it all?

oh, yes
you are dawn itself
if you are awake
you will be born burning
billions of mornings
you
and the earth

3.

and if you aren't awake
then you will burn yourself out

becoming flame within ice
wind within wind
retribution within crime
death within death

standing on this hill
the moment petals fall
there are still stars in the sky
you're not coming back
an embryonic deer lies fallow
so you think

to be myself and only myself

can't I wake and go
out into the world
as one human being?
just like this
without any blessings to share or bestow
only holding onto the turbulence at boiling point?
you are the darkness
tracing seasons
petals falling
to the bottom of what—justice?

who are you?
you are the universe

4.

while the cosmos is whispering in your ear
you're not asking for *reconstruction*
you seek *rehabitation*
you have declared to the ocean
it's not to *return*, but to make it *new*

such words remind me:
the rotation of the stars

Abandoned Fukushima

Abandoned Fukushima on this hushed rainy night
within the hush, there is a tenderness
a cold wind jostles a swing in the city park
pushing the rusty chains back and forth

Abandoned Fukushima on this hushed rainy night
within the hush, my mother carries a deep compassion
as she rushes through the wet streets
the small marshes are silent in falling rain

Abandoned Fukushima on this hushed rainy night
within the hush, a husky sigh as a boy drifts off to sleep
on the back of his eyelids, he sees wild horses in a Tibetan field
at the neighbor's house, camellias are falling in a rush

Abandoned Fukushima on this hushed rainy night
within the hush, in the freezing cold, there is the first draft of a poem
with promises whirling on am empty page
in the next town, the vending machines are all sold out

Abandoned Fukushima on this hushed rainy night
within the hush, who cries
remembering those who have left this world
keeping their memory alive
an ocean rests on these eyelids

Abandoned Fukushima on this hushed rainy night, a small train station
a forsaken ticket gate   a pristine train waiting to depart
on the midnight platform
what could be footsteps pass

Abandoned Fukushima on this hushed rainy night, a river flows,
birds are talking about their exploits in the sky
they spread their wings over the spinning earth
could it be that our dreams are about to start

so hushed this rainy night
our souls sleep in the darkness

hushed rain and a glimmering dawn   the rain stops
hush hushed   fallen over by light
morning breaks with an infant's first cry
these arms cradling the baby

and suddenly, I become a father

oh, a child with eyes open
your journey through the rainy night
oh, child of Fukushima
you are newborn

thank you for arising into the world
this is your dawn

January 1, 2021

late December, sunset, combing Soma beach
I picked up a spiral shell
now it's dawn, New Year's Day

  without warning the tide rose
  with an eerie stillness

  soon it was higher than 9 meters
  a pitch dark monster wave
    life and death and tears and fish

  and wind and boats and cars

  and downed electric poles

  the nuclear power plants failed on the 12th and 14th of March, 2011

  scores of people evacuated

  the sea called my name
  frightened
  I pretended not to hear

  can time crash over us in waves?

  did I really not hear?

  in its spiral, can a seashell hold
  a decade of memories?
  in the palm of my hand,
  I felt a chill

*

"More shaking. Such big tremors.
We've continued to expect big aftershocks
and now it seems like we're in it again."
                          (3/16/2011)

*

ahhhh
quaking
still now
we live
day by day

*

 "A missing person becomes a valid missing person
after a report is filed. Without a report,
they cannot be a valid missing person.
So, is a missing person a missing person?"
                          (3/16/2011)

MINESAWA NORIKO
tr. Eric Margolis

Departure from Perpignan

In one railroad car
many languages whisper amongst each other
on a sleepy
midday.

The long distance train at last
starts to speed up,
loosening the live coals
heavy in the passengers' hearts.
The sky
belts out summer.

The train window is damp with sunflower oil.
The horizon, curling by in the bow of a horse's stomach
is sprinkled by the laughter
of Maria and the others
with all their skin colors
and the smell of flowers,
ripening like sun-tanned song.

Those who just got off the train
arrived among blooming camellias
at a deep pool of dozing.
Whispers of *bon voyage*
in Spanish.

When the shadow of the border,
gathering in pitchers of water,
reddish,
stuffs its cheeks with
cigarettes and
chocolate and

pronounces
the south, in
the burning wind
of August:
eyelids.

With the Summer Rain

As if chasing after
fallen flower petals,
the rain at dawn
soaks the map of summer in my dream.

No longer
will I again visit
that far
southern town.
After the rain
the silent morning slope was fragrant
with jasmine, lilac, and rose,
and the shadows of butterflies just out of sight.
Human life
learns to sing the names of things just as fleeting—
and then another moment's journey
even if quickly forgotten.

Instead of counting the things that I've lost
I'll remember the strength of the scent of scattering
jasmine, lilac, and rose,
and even on rainy mornings
continue to open my dark window.

I pray that the sound of rain
from those gentle days
in the faraway town of flowers
where I walked just once
with you who I can still meet in dreams now
becomes, above my damp eyes,
the beginning
of a brand new summer.

Cancellation

On moonless days
the cicada wings
fallen by my pillow—
letters from a person who can no longer reply
forevermore.
I touched
their blurred cancellation postmarks
and smelled the southern vineyards
we visited one time.

When faraway stars cross
once more
the shadows of the green fruit in my dreams
that keep swaying in the early autumn dusk
along with my body
will surely be gone from this world.

On moonless nights
I'm still unable to clearly remember
the place on the southern hill
or the name of the constellation
illuminating the cheek next to mine.

The chill of the shoulder
I touched that day
melts away
into cicadas' phantom cries
in the unseeable moonlight
like the final postmark
cancellation.

FUJITA YUKIHIRO
tr. Matthew Guay

Zero

There is nothing here
Neither any doubt
Nor any kind of you.

You and
I are
Zero.

So
I can say
Nothing more,
If I did
Part of my mind would
Make me stop
And that
Wouldn't do you
Any good.

If we pull back time
Just a little further
I and these words
Could be made
As if they had never been.

But you
Will inevitably
Return
There
Even if it hurts.

There
The regular you
With
Another
Me.

Then
Us
Will be gone.

Subway

Two girls pushing
A girl in a wheelchair
Head for the front of the platform.
Soon a train arrives
The conductor uses a large metal plate
To help the wheel chair board the train.
A kind looking man of middle years
Observing the scene
Soon finds himself joining in
Helping the wheelchair safely onto the carriage.
Grinning, he remarks
"Looks like you are all set there."
The girls don't respond
An old man
Seeing the girls board
Offers his seat saying
"Please sit here."
Wordlessly, the girls sit down
The silence continues
For a while.
The girls begin chatting in hushed voices
Plans for the day slip in and out of the silence.
The train pulls up at the fifth station down the line
Without so much as a glance back at the man who helped them,
The girls exit the train
This time with only the help of the conductor.
The train starts moving
The middle-aged man sits down in a now vacated seat
Embarrassment flush on his face
The old man next to him
Does his best
not to look.

Dry Ice

A sudden visit of light
Joy with no superior
My body crystalized from suffering and impatience
Eviscerated.

Desire to bathe in the light
For each step closer
The light dims fainter
The past seduces me with a feverish sickness but,

My unseen future
Calling the goddess of fate
Hands me over with a smile and tears.

"Never put
 Dry ice in the water.
 Bathe in it as long as it lasts."

Self-Reflection Locker

The self-reflection locker
The cold locker that
Made you,
Isn't that a refrigerator?

The long unopened locker
Peering inside
A gift box of fine confectionery.
Before you can remember when
Your eyes process
An expiration date from the distant past.
In the background
The audience looks on.

Despite the date,
This is your self-reflection locker
The contents of the box should
Still edible
You proclaim.
The many eyes
Gasp
However,
It would be rude to......

How many people are in this room?
One, two, three......
Yes
One per person
Behave yourselves.
When asked who wants one
Everyone should silently raise their hand.

The many eyes
Fill with fear.

Even so
This is your self-reflection locker
There is every reason to return to it
Then everyone will come meet you
Thus
You must eat first.

The food looks like
It takes courage
To bring to your mouth.
Your right hand commits a heroic act,
A sudden and tragic invasion
Tasting produces
A high-speed rejection.
Screams rebound
Turning around,
There you can see the many eyes
Filled with derision.

The still open
Cold locker
Over there,
Isn't that a refrigerator?

That You

That you
Absorbed into
Another world
You surely
Are there.

Intellectual fascination
That breaks your heart in two
Absolute excitement
That sears your skin
Intense agitation.

The place I am at is
The given "present"
That everyone knows.
Its dry current
Completely destroyed by
The one further than my memories,
That
You

KISAKA RYO
tr. Taylor Mignon

Kusa-Kanmuri

Holding a pen,
I press the receiver to my ear.

"There's a line going across.
A small mark goes through it, then another…
It, uh, looks   like a hat!"
Taylor explains in English.
Not the romanized letters
but in *kanji* we exchange addresses,
between Chiba and Saitama
now we are in the middle of
                    forming the Chinese character…
If he knew
what kusa-kanmuri was
that would be it,
and yet
putting little marks on the horizontal line,
the pen point lends an etching, something hat-like
and it looks like many things
so we laugh in tandem.

At mid-chuckle
I get the idea of the form
relying on Taylor's phonetic reading,
I   am all alone now
getting into one ration of Japanese.
Beyond this good time
like a line tearing in two.
A hat of kusa-kanmuri
with the unfinished etching at hand.

A Midsummer Happening

My cat returns home
with a wall-lizard seized in its mouth.

Already, it's tailless at the root.
Even though detached by itself
how sudden that must be for a tail!

Cut off like a severed box car
by a phone call a few minutes ago,

I am eyeing it.

MARTHA NAKAMURA
tr. Kendall Heitzman

A Discovery

My maternal grandmother's house was in Miyagi, on a fairly high hill in the city of Kesennuma. At the bottom of her street, so steep we careened down it as we ran, was a place from which we could look out at the ocean below. My family lived in inland Saitama, so to me the screeching seagulls and the sea air that brought a smell like a garbage bin belonged to another world.

My mother would take my older brother and me to Grandma's house in early August, and we would stay until the end of the Obon festival, after the fires had been lit to guide the spirits away again. The bullet train tickets cost so much, my father didn't go along. This was our annual tradition until I entered elementary school.

As soon as we arrived at Grandma's we always wanted to go straight to the sea. We could see it right there in front of us, but to get to the shore by car was a ten-minute drive down. Even so, unless there was a thunderstorm, we would go down to the beach every day. The summers are cool in Kesennuma. You almost never have a day when the sun is blazing. On the shore, dulled underfoot by the thick clouds overhead, my mother and aunt would talk about everything and nothing. My older brother would bob in the surf, suspended between his orange floaties. I would play in the sand in my pink swimsuit. No one came to the beach besides us. The people who lived in the area feared going into the ocean too close to Obon. *The dead will pull us under*, they said.

Pieces of shells, shards of blue glass, chips of dried-out wood that stick to your fingers, plastic bags crumpled like old people's skin. That's what lurked in the sand on the beach. When I looked up, I saw my brother staring off over the waves. My mother and my aunt were seated on the steps that led down to the shore, their native accent burbling along in its peculiar way.

I worked so hard to create a lake, hard by the ocean. I clenched my toes to gingerly make my way across the shifting sand that threatened to suck me under at any moment. With my little yellow shovel, I scrape-scraped my way down into the beach. Using a red bucket that long ago housed a pet crawfish, I scooped water from the ocean and poured it into my lake in a sudden deluge.

Sloooorsh.

The muddy water swirled around—not something you see very often in actual lakes. Without even waiting for the white froth to swirl out to the sides, the black sand at the bottom greedily gulped down the liquid. The last of the pool disappeared from sight with a *whish*. And I would go back to the ocean to scoop more water.

One time, I was making a lake as usual. My little shovel skidded across the surface of a scrap of paper. Instinctively, I pulled it out. It was perfectly white, as though it had just been placed there. I sat down in the sand, as warm as a person's touch, and spread the paper out.

> We cannot choose
> how we will die.
> Death is something that
> is thrust upon us.

The tall, thin characters had been written so that any child could understand, with a black ballpoint pen. The paper was damp, but the lines were still crisp.

I folded the paper up again, the way I had found it, and returned it to the beach from whence it came. I patted down the sand with my palms. Then, for whatever reason, I wanted to dig it up again. But no matter how far down I dug, the scrap of paper was nowhere to be found.

The Back Fell

In the back of my throat is a rank tanuki box. If I keep my silence, its lid opens up. In the night-world inside the box, the tanuki always keeps a bonfire going. There are two boulders by it; he has planted himself on one. He shoves sticks forked at one end like bird's legs into the fire, seemingly annoyed at the task. The firewood belches its way into ash, and the sparks that rise up die out before I ever get a bead on them. I look at this tanuki who doesn't resist his lot, who seems to absorb the reddish-orange glow cast on his face. His world is surrounded on three sides by mountains practically looming over him. A tanuki pup stands at the spine of one, yawping on and on and pulling stars from the sky. Out of the steam, the pup casts a line and reels in the stars he likes.

"We become aware of things, and then comes the fall." Without lifting his face from the flames, the tanuki starts to tell the story of the Old Fallen Man. A master woodcutter used to be here, a fellow who liked his cedars as wide across as he was. He would put his back up against one and whirl his baubles made only of water itself. Then he chopped into the tree from three directions, and felled it by pushing against it with his back.

A month ago, the woodcutter bobbled his water. Down it all sloshed, forming a river. The tanuki hurried there to help, he tells me, but the woodcutter was already floating in a little boat. The wooden vessel was nearly rotted out; sand and water sloshed in its bilge. It still bobbed on the surface, but it was already saying, *we are fallen*. The gunwale of the boat scraped up some of the foulness of the mountain. The stench threatened to burn my throat. "We become aware of things, and then comes the fall. But how vulgar to gradually become aware. The closest you can get to being human is to have that sudden moment of clarity." The woodcutter drifted off to a place he could no longer be reached. When he disappeared from sight, the river at last ran dry.

"I will drive my blade into the mountains, then back up against them and topple them. The fell will fall in three directions." The tanuki, as always, is keeping the bonfire going. Up on the spine, a little voice yawps *on, on*. Another star falls from the sky. I realize it's a bone. If I open my mouth, the lid to the box will close, so I sit and stare at the tanuki. He splays his fingertips out to the heat, and doesn't so much as blink.

KEIJIRO SUGA
tr. Jordan A. Y. Smith

Sichuan / Four Rivers

<u>The river that flows east</u> conjures a slumber in violet,
Its dozing ripples barely concealing a parched awakening,
Against the angle of your shoulders break murky ripples dyed in bright tears,
Alternating with the glittering indigo shadows of lifeforce,
The slope of your shoulders traces wave crests, blazing trails through sunlight,
When the river dolphins swim right through ascending sun, huge
Koi and catfish swish feebly after them,
Staying in the wake of this gathering, a turtle trudges through its beloved mud,
An awakening the likes of which the world has yet to see,
The turtle's subjectivity lends it great agility,
My own endeavor just to describe the animal's and your own soporific
Superficial sliding over the water surface,
So, let sleep slip away, give up on it,
When you set out swimming, I'll swim after,
Drinking in the sunlit ripples your gliding shoulders scatter
I sent word to the king of the koi, reigning over the river: it's time to settle things,
A message transcending species, transcending time,
Never erring on its path toward arrival, somewhere, to someone,
And look, the river dolphins jump spraying rainbows—
It's your love and it's oblivion
An ocean of awakening, just over there

<u>The river that flows west</u> washes away the written word
So I cut my hair short and splash right in,
Swim! Swim! my dog tells me,
A Newfoundland, the enormous swimming breed,
But the letters spread out dazzlingly over the water surface
Glinting like dark silver koi swimming ever faster,
As the river pours into a ravine, a Lorelei perches atop a rock on the riverbank,
A gorgeous Nordic blonde girl, naked and singing away,
The song instills the letters with the power of real fish, and they begin to leap,

Her hair seems to net all the letters used to form the lyrics she sings,
Yes, to the baptism, yes, to the lexicon,
Yes, to the lamentation, yes, to the luminescence,
Amazing, I mutter, secretly aroused,
I swear a new oath to search for the terms of an unrecorded language,
If I can harness her power, the labor of compilation will be all too easy,
Beyond that, it's just a matter of classifying seawater from fresh water,
Fishing up the letters before they're washed into the saltwater zone,
Yet it's not a task I must do to perfection,
The words rust,
And as they rust, they are
Rendered as eternal as a dictionary of iron

The river that flows north aims for the hunting grounds,
Parting from, then clinging to, mountains and critter-filled forests
As it snakes its way through the flats,
Rather, the river is mother of the land here,
On top of this thick layer of peat,
Dwell the deer and other larger deer, they say,
In this river, I do not swim but ride in a seal-skin kayak
Also snaking its way slowly downstream
Careful to avoid the whirlpools around the fallen trees along the riverbanks,
The shadows of enormous sky-dancing birds cross my eyelids, eclipsing the sun,
At this latitude, noon finds the sky an indigo densely packed with stars,
The constellations are a hunter's mnemonic, the sky a notebook,
An album of beasts who sacrificed their lives for the sake of humans,
From there, as the fresh crescent moon dips toward the lake—
What could that be? …in the transparent depths countless sunken skeletons
In a cemetery of the deer, a layer so silent no poem or song can penetrate,
Within it, my kayak starts spinning
The sounds of water, the music to a dirge,
I greet and bid goodbye to the deer,
Deer, thank you, deer,
What a lively kind of loneliness

<u>The river that flows south</u> some call the river of forgetting,
As I swim across its surface, countless fruits splashing down around me,
Spraying rains of plump droplets
On my head when I swim breaststroke, and on my face with backstroke,
Alligators by the score, but they don't scare me,
They are all as small as my pinky fingers,
And piranhas all around, but they don't scare me either,
Because ultimately their appetites are for physical flesh
And the more I swim the more metaphysical my existence becomes —
A river with this kind of powerful effect, what can it mean?
True enough, the electric eels are dangerous,
Suddenly I can hear an electric guitar solo in the distance,
A figment heard, as one says, 'with ears to the sky,'
Unsettling image—ears floating in the sky!
Were it not for that, I'd grab up all the soursop and alligator-skinned avocados
And steadily ingest their nutrition so I could swim forever,
The clingy, murky olive green water coats my skin and my spirit in velvet,
So freed from existence itself, carefree as an eel,
Every last chain of karma fades to the farside of oblivion,
And when I open my eyes underwater,
I see myself swimming

TANAKA IKUKO

tr. Miho Kinnas & Shelly Bryant

In the Wind of Bleached Memory

One day, after the wind, my father was on the battlefield
One day, after the wind, my father was a returned soldier
He came home to the dirt yard of the narrow land in the mountains
His body was thin and his face tinted yellow
I peeked at him from behind my mother, I was told

He, in my memory, was always sick
An egg, he ate, threw up and lost in diarrhea
A piece of fish, he ate, threw up and lost in diarrhea
His body diminished
One day as he hurt his spine in the forest
One day he lost consciousness under the falling tree

He didn't talk about the battlefield
When the rough wind blew
he saluted with a stern expression
shouted, stammered and I heard the slapping of the cheeks in the dark
On another day whatever the wind blew
he raised his hand high with a chess piece between the fingers
then thwacked it down and that made him smile
He fished a trout he kept in the pond and that made him smile

And then, with Huntington's disease, he grew thinner and his hands trembled
And then, he was stung by an October bee and died at the age of fifty eight

One day, in the wind of the bleached memory
I was a middle school student
'Democracy' was brand new
'America' was brand new
I stood by the window and my father said to me
'Girls are better off not reading newspapers'
I wondered what he was still fighting against

His voice was very low
It has been sixty years
The voice and meaning fade away
I stand in the dirt yard — nothing has changed there —
I stand by the window where I faced my father
In the space between the feeble light and the warmth of blood
I place the printed word 'Peace'
In the light, in one sliver of light,

the image of my father doesn't come together
because it doesn't — I think
I will carry with me the space by the opaque window
of the abandoned house
The eyes of the battlefield seemed gentle
They might have been lonely just as
the wind, the light and the shadow are

Sixty Years

From the invisible sky
the snow falls, is falling, has fallen
Sixty years, it has been
If it snows all day
vomit and gunshots will turn white
the peaceful window and tragic news will also turn
in no time, they will be buried all white
Which alley might this be?
Which house might this eave belong to?
The snowy corner I take is familiar yet somehow foreign
Walking toward or away
I am inside the door at a small clinic
On the reclined chair
a diseased tooth is pulled out
My lips are numb and this is how I pass the end of my sixty years
As I sit pushed up by the rising chair the white mask informs:
   These seven front teeth came in when you were seven
   They have small cavities and I brush them with fluoride
What's going on? The snow dances!
and with the sudden bright light I am seven
I eat chestnuts with Asako, an evacuee from the city
I hear the hymns my aunt from Hiratsuka sings
We had no way of knowing that soon
an atomic bomb would fall and we would lose the war
in that house that had been
From the invisible sky on my way home, too
Watching the river flow from the bridge
Watching the snow melt into the water
I stop for no reason
and it deepens right there
the bubbles that hit the rock turn white like snowdrop buds
I turn and face the sixty-year old eyes fading
It is said night falls fast on a snowy day

White Tune

Scattered, my snow in the village
          over the roof and the rooms dormant for so long
          over the the tree in the backyard not even a little bird flutters
with the storm of wind and snow
as if the silence begins to speak
softly, snow, fall softly and stay

Distanced by the window panes
aimed with a white beam the long ago date
a piece of mid-winter catches the light and pirouettes
a room under the roof, its lantern lights
Startled with the flash on my father's winter soldier hat
It is the shape of the strange country on its frozen continent
It is the shape of eating from the steel pot my mother polished
Turned sideways from each other in yesterday's time
Something like love, something that cries no more

Old-time cells must be hidden
Someone strums between the sky and the earth
What had happened repeats on
Endlessly arriving the white tune
Only a buried ear listens

SONIC NURSE
tr. Jordan A. Y. Smith

Why Aren't You Stopping the Camera?

Please listen, I need to whine..
I have a deadline.
That my diagnosis with an incurable disease and the pronouncement that same day
    that two of my friends started dating both to me carried equal weight was I
    guess because I am abnormally optimistic.
Usually
I would have cried more, gotten angrier,
Been unable to accept it.
But I've been struggling with this theme since way back.
On my fourteenth birthday, my father
Told me,
"Your mother's disease is muscular dystrophy."
"Your mother's disease is incurable.".
"Your mother's disease is genetically inherited."
"There's a good chance you'll get it, too."

I am nothing like my mother,
But I'll get the same disease
People didn't believe me because my body looks strong.
They just laughed it off in easy disbelief.
But
I'm the one who wishes it was a lie.
I'm the one who wants to laugh it off
Sometimes I wonder if it really could be a lie.
But that confuses me,
I feel ashamed,
I feel guilt,
Like I'm missing out on something very important about life.
Like I'm still dreaming.
A hazy sensation running through the veins in back of my head.

I was nothing like my mother,
But I got the same disease.
She was foul-mouthed, a good driver, strong-minded, down with subculture, cool.
And me: quiet, helpless, clueless.
We had nothing in common when I was little
But finally, I've become like her!
I'm not happy about that.
In my head, I accuse her, "Why did you have a baby, you idiot?"
I wanted to see my own children.
I wanted to meet them.
Give me a break, mother.
It's selfish.
I'm sorry. But turn off that camera.
I'm putting an end to this here.
Why don't you turn off the camera?
Why do you still think you can love?
That you have some kind of love in you that chews and suckles?
A father's square-ironed face issuing a soundless congratulations.
A face I'll never forget.
I never saw my mother smile.
Because she had no facial muscles
I long pretended like I knew love,
Pretended that love had been planted inside,
Who will smile at me and inspire me to smile back?
Whose mirror have I been reflecting?
Afraid to touch your hand because I'm afraid that if I do,
You'll melt like snow,
I'm too scared to go near
It doesn't piss me off when people say *Poor thing!*
Or *She's struggling to stay strong!*
But I won't let you say I was wrong.
I won't let you say I must be lying.
I'll live my life the way I want to, thanks.
So turn off that camera.
Because from here on,
I will be doing the writing.

Give Me Sunlight

Give me some sun like a needle jab
Give me the sun on my knees, because it's winter
Slowly, gently.
But when you pierce the skin, do it decisively.
Like when you break the lid of drink-box latte with your straw,
Like when you use a hypodermic needle to suck out the blood.
It's cold, so give me the sun as gently as if you were kneeling,

Give me some sun
Give me vivid colors, vitamin hues, to cheer me up,
How foolish it is
To pretend like you're keeping lock-step with others in order not to feel inferior.
Why can I always only slander myself and never give myself concrete advice?
I take occasional pride in just being alive, undaunted
By the command to die echoing in my ears every day,
Simultaneously aware that the feeling of superiority
Comes only from striving to survive my own insanity.
No matter how much sex you have in the realm of dreams,
Reality cannot even get into that country you live in.
If you don't travel, the story gets no beginning.
Hop the bullet train.
There's no reason to go out, let's go out.
Just sway with the rapid train and eventually we'll find that treasure.
We don't need the heaters.
Sunshine is plenty.
Here I notice the sun, the one light in the park that is not artificial.
If a poet were to venture out, wouldn't they just get angry and dismayed at the world's worthlessness?
People who have it easy say, "You shouldn't think of yourself as being so precious."
And yet, I pray helplessly, with abandon.

May I be worthy.
May I be a unique, precious human.
Since it slips off my lap each time I stand,
I want sunshine that will never fall off.
I want the sunshine that will never fall off.
I want you to shine it firmly on my lap so that it will not fall off.
Over the summer, an appalling amount of sun dust has clung to my skin
Its particles turning my skin a loathsome color.
The sun is dyeing me an unflattering color.
Even though it's only the good parts of the sun I want to absorb.

The more they love me,
The more they realize how useless my existence is.
Because there is nothing more loveable
Than something useless.
I will drink as many cups of coffee as I can.
As to why I don't just discard
The black and white impurities afloat in my poetry,
Only the oddly overgrown banyan tree can tell me.
Which way would you go if you were a poet on an adventure?
I'll refill my black coffee again because I can't beat the exhaustion.

Sorry I've been sitting here all this time.
We stop at the next station.

SAN SIMON
tr. Jordan A. Y. Smith

Moving Point A

Do you remember me?

From around page 8 of the math textbook

I was the one sent on an errand to buy three apples for 130 yen and five oranges for
    70 yen.
Yes, Takashi. That's me.

I would like you to listen to what happened to me in the days following that.

After the errand, I met a strange creature.
A creature that moved swiftly.
He looked like an angel and beeped.
I named him Moving Point A.

One day I fell in love. Or actually, I didn't know the word "love" yet.
What name should I have given that feeling?

Little Richard sang "Tutti Frutti,"
but as for me, I couldn't think of any words.

Mari, a girl in my class, had big, round eyes like a French doll.
And into those eyes, I fell.

There were seven of us boys and girls playing together.
I was paired with Mari, but one of my friends started to poke fun at me.

Wooh, hoo! You two look so happy together! Are you going out? Is it true love???

I wasn't too ruffled about it, but I had to play it tough.
Shit, as if! With her big ol' bug eyes, who would like her?

…I meant it as a gag.
But when Mari heard those words, her eyes became lakes.

After that, Mari stopped playing with our group.

Some time later, after school one day in December, I found a letter in my locker:

> *Takashi, I'm sorry for the sudden notice,*
> *but I'm moving to Paris.*
>
> *You know, I…I liked you, Takashi.*
> *That's why I was shocked when you called me bug eyes.*
>
> *I'm taking a 3 PM flight today.*
> *If you ever come to Paris, let me know.*
>
> *Sayonara,*
>
> *Mari*

I became a scarecrow.

My Tutti Frutti melted away,
and went splatty watty on the ground.

Even if I leave now, there's no way I could make it to the airport.

Just then, I remembered him.
That's right — Moving Point A!

I went to find him.

"Point A! I want to see Mari one more time.
Please take me to the airport!"

Point A moved swiftly to my side, turned his back to me, and hollered:

"Hop on!"

A gust of wind blew around us, and he carried me away at breakneck speed.

Now here's the problem!

Mari left 50 minutes ago in a car going 100 kilometers per hour.
Moving Point A is heading for the airport 180 km away traveling at 250 km/h.
How many minutes will Takashi and Moving Point A take to catch up with Mari?

Or… will they not be able to catch up in time?
Are the words that passed between them never to bloom again?

I'll leave the correct answer to your imagination.

However,
The little right hand that was clutching the 1,000-yen notes around page 8 of the
    math textbook is now clutching an international flight ticket with a few wrinkles.

Honey on Pancakes

Honey on pancakes
yummy fluffy happy
friendly smiley

Little Butter Dude
acting punky on my pancakes
Slips around, frowning *Leave me alone*

But eeeeeveryone knows
Smiley smiley smiley
Drool dripping onto the frying pan

Honey on pancakes

Crowded TV screens
Makeup-caked grannies
Screaming about density

It is not my fault
We have no problem.
The bad people are over there

Hotcakes get hotter
I Scream, You Scream

If you've got time to scoop ice cream
You should be eating our honey

The honey factory manager is smiling too

Feeling all flustery frustrated?
Try falling in love with someone

Love tastes like lemon honey
Until you lose it, it's Technicolor

When you realize your love is lost
It's a black and white movie, Jim Jarmusch
No detectable taste or smell

When you realize you can't detect it,
Adulthood begins

It's not about the number of wrinkles
It's not about the number of words

It's about memorizing, learning, working,
Playing, sleeping, kneeling,
When memories wettened
With impulsive tears
Spill over pancakes,
That's the flavor of someone's first love

Round and round and round-abouting
Tiger turns butter, butter turns tiger
The sea gave birth to life
Life raised cake flour
That became lunch for
The turtle who carries the stars

KATAYAMA SAYURI
tr. Jordan A. Y. Smith

Just. So. Tired.

A part-time job it's hard to tell even your best friends about
It's good money! But boring AF.
If I could just kill my heart, I could get pretty woohah about it, I got this,
But actually that's pretty tough to pull off.
The guilt that konbini impulse-buys used to arouse is pretty much extinguished.
I've grown numb and numb-er, but there is a part I carefully guard from going
    numb.

I put my hair up
and sink into lonely
On the train home, I played a girly romance video game
and got bored inside ten minutes
I drank some booze so I could sing
a song that let me belt out shallow stuff

It feels like cement's stuck in my throat   so tired   so tired
It feels like cement's stuck in my throat   so tired   so tired   so tired

That part-time job I can't even tell my best friends about —
I'm quitting this month, it's deathly boring
Used to yearn for a lifestyle
that afforded shopping sprees at PARCO or LUMINE or wherever.
I love standing at bookstores browsing JUMP comics, but this week's issue sucks.
I've been faking it week in and week out. Let's just pay the cashier and checkout.

Don't fuckin run away from me.

Can't find anything fun, so I try eating something I hate.
Those *things* you never leave home without, dissolve one in your booze
Flirting with depression isn't depression, but the real deal cuts deep.
The nurse's rooms. The truancy.
Each day alive is a victory, even if you crawl through on your knees.

If you crawl to the end of the day and survive, you'll win.
If you make it to the end,
Then you, too.
You, too,
Can experience defeat.

It feels like cement's stuck in my throat   so tired   so tired
It feels like cement's stuck in my throat   so tired   so tired
It feels like cement's stuck in my throat   so tired   so tired
It feels like cement's stuck in my throat   so tired   so tired   so tired
So tired   tired   tired

I'm wiped out.

That part-time job I can't even tell my best friends about —
    I'm not going in today.

I am. Just. So. Tired.

Man in the Dunes

Bad men are still as attractive now as they ever were.
I'm almost sick of it.
Mounting debts ignored, aimless travels, womanizing…
But 26 is a bit too soon

I've been working and working, but can't get a break,
There was a song for you too
Let's talk, off in one corner of the library,
And I'd just listen.
But I felt you were my friend.

I wish there were laws to protect only you,
Because I haven't even shared my whole story with you
"I was born in a town where it snows"… "There was no more war, you know"

I too was born in a town where it snows.
But there was no more war, you know

Supermarket Fantasy

Welcome, valued shopper! Thank you for visiting us today. Do you have a point card with us?

When he got into the checkout line at my register, I wanted to knock over all the customers' baskets, scattering the contents all over the place, and run off screaming. The victim bears the memories until death, while the aggressor gets to forget, or so I hear about the anatomy of bullying, and true to this formula, I remember. He lived in the same little burg as my parents, among the populace of which he was the number one person I wanted to murder.

Bullying in elementary school is just horseplay taken too far, hahahaaa—anyone who laughs it off like this is the type to spew emoji cacophonies all over FaceBook or Instagram.

And *he* is exactly that type. He can fucking die. I deal with the customers one by one, expertly, and he draws steadily nearer. *The line at my register is still pretty long, dude, still time to cut over to another line… Do not come near me. Or at least act like you don't know me.* Alerts blare in my head, *Act like you don't know me act like you don't know me act like you don't know me.* But the dumb fuck's eyes get bigger and he throws his hand up like *heeeeyyy!* Just as my brain is about to issue the command to say, "Who the fuck are you?", before I can, my head nods automatically in return. We are cashier and customer, so it's natural enough. *Die!* He has a child with him. He has a family, a house. Why? Why does he get to just live his life, leaving others to bear the wounds he inflicted in their hearts forever?

In my parents' village, the locals typically all hear every detail of everyone's family structure, jobs, families they marry into, and places of higher education kids enter, so I knew that he'd got married and become a father, of the fact that he built a house in our local neighborhood. But no one would know that I dropped out of college after eight years in Tokyo, came back, and quietly picked up a part-time job at this supermarket. I am sure the neighbors have seen me staggering to the convenience store 1.3 kilometers away during the daytime to buy booze, but no one's ever mentioned it. The Katayama family's daughter is always acting fishy during the daytime. What a disgrace to the family! To my family, I am a disgrace. I am a stain on my family's honor. No proper job, contributing nothing, her very existence is nothing but a burden. Precisely meeting the definition of a "parasite." No need to even tell Grandma that Sayuri is back from Tokyo. No one will be rejoicing at her return. But I don't care. Because I'm not like you fucks. I have tons of friends in Tokyo, people who appreciate me, and even a second home. In Tokyo, I have another personality, loved by many. So I don't care if I'm socially dead here, if I don't have a driver's license or a car, or even if I have no friends whatsoever to hang with. I have Tokyo. If I can go back to Tokyo again, I will once again be brimming with vitality. I have no idea why, though I am just one little human, in this little burg, I'm supposed to care so much about my home, my family, my reputation. Normally, it would be nothing to worry about. It's painful. And it's my hometown, so I'm supposed to love it.

I scan the items at a speed that doesn't give him time to talk to me, give him the change and the receipt, and finally I manage to take a deep breath. It's not wise to rehash the past. I get that, but whatever, I'm fine with being a pain in the ass. I don't care if people cluck, *Why must you eternally bitch and moan about bygones? People like that become criminals*. If I don't say something, no one else will, so it will be as if nothing happened, so whether ten years pass or twenty, I will be here rehashing it. I will say it. You *fucking hear* me? That newly built house, where you repeatedly abused me, a child powerless to fight back, and you violated me over and over again, as I stand here today, know goddamn well that I set the whole fucking thing on fire.

Thank you very much! We hope you'll come back to shop with us again soon!

ENDO HITSUJI
tr. Nakagawa Junnosuke

Sunset

Fish are forming lines
And surging this way,
Sunset
From somewhere, the smell of something burnt

"It's nice and grilled," the neighbor said,
"No, it's just grilled on one side," I said
"It has to be flipped over," he repeated,
"You mean, my life?" I replied, with an unsavory chill,

Putting the neighbor's kindness and my ignorance
In the plastic bag at AEON supermarket,
The deep shadows stretch alongside the rows of fish

The neighbor grilled, nothing but Atka mackerel, and we ate it together,
We sipped something like beer, then I apologized to him for what happened on the
    way home,
The neighbor played dumb, asking "What for?", the night had come.

Eutychus

I may witness it every now and then
People deliberately, or
Unintentionally
Throwing their lives away
I,
with clear visibility
And absolute eyesight
Will witness that scene

However, what about their discarded bodies?
In those bodies,
If the internalized sense of sight is working normally
If the sight of people who cross boundaries
Is not narrowing

*

In the middle of a certain night, I witnessed:
At my familiar home train station, at the very end of the row,
I sat in the chair, throwing my legs out toward that boundary
Beyond which trains passed at breakneck speed

I saw a woman

Her legs covered with a beige cloth
Swaying unsteadily,
She wore a suit, had chestnut hair

The glossy high-heels and jaundiced legs,
The air of a spiritual awakening, and her head hanging,
Like a pendulum, swinging,

She is looking down, so I cannot visually recognize her face,
Her knees shake,
Even made the tips of her hair sway slightly,
Before I was could walk toward the woman

A blue conductor appeared and
Warned her,
"That's a dangerous place to stand!"
She seemed surprised as her face lifted
And her eyes flew open
Then, she dropped her head as if ashamed,
Stood up, and sent out resonations of the forceless sound of high-heeled footsteps,
As she exited the station through the ticket gate

*

On the first night of that week,
The adolescent Eutychus, exhausted from work,
Sat by the open window
And listened carefully to the voices of the gathering
Whereas Eutychus's belly was stuffed
The orange tint of his face deepened
His eyes drowsy, arms and legs drained,
Under the unconsciousness, voices were hidden in mist,
The core of his being shifted off-balance, and from the third floor, Eutychus
Silently fell

Eutychus's body seemed lifeless
However,
Paul cradled him in his arms,
Though the facts said the boy had died, Paul announced,
"Trouble not yourselves, for his life is in him,"
That wording made
Eutychus shake and awaken

*

That woman with beige hair
Could have died

At that scene
She might have been subconscious
That's right
She was subconsciously forced
To commit suicide

Eutychus
Went to the congregation to cure his mind
But his body was too exhausted
And he was subconsciously forced to commit suicide

I witnessed
On the platform of the station, by the description of the Acts of the Apostles
The scene of the person subconsciously forced to commit suicide

---

* Eutychus: a young man who appears in the Acts of the Apostles
in chapter 20, verses 7-12.

Already the Future

Looking at the cloudless sky,
makes me miss the clouds

Looking at a beautiful realist painting,
Makes me want to see something abstract, like a lump of heat

Reading a poem that shines all the way to its margins
Makes we want to hear a reading where every silent pause robs my breath

The grass is always greener on the other side of the fence, so I go there
But then, the grass I'd been on before starts looking even greener

Everybody is stuck in their glory days
And they continue going back and forth towards the future

When you hesitate to look back at the past, it's already the future,
When you repeat the days of sloth, it's already the future

The days of boring chores,
And the joyous night you achieved your goal, both are the future

There is no now,
Forever, future
The past melts and softens
Starts to shine as future memories

Now is forever the future,
Perpetual future,
The past spreads over the sky
And look — it has brought us perfectly white clouds.

KOORI HIRONOBU
tr. Jordan A. Y Smith

The Forgotten Song

Swaying along down the road, a sightseeing bus
Took us out to an old port town.
This is the port of Shimotsui, facing the sea between Japan's main island and
    Shikoku,
That once flourished with traffic from
the shipping route from central Japan, its ships at the mercy of wind and tide.

We, the happy tourists,
Led by a guide,
Walk the streets of the old town
Listening
To an old song from the old glory days of this port

♪ Shimotsui harbor, easy to yo-yo in and out,
Sail right in, with tailwinds or headwinds
The wind that blows from the sea
Sweeping the silhouettes to the surface,
A distant murmur

Beneath the dark roof,
through the window
that inhales the ocean breezes

There, a forgotten memory
A dozen brothels and tatami rooms for rent
in the distance
I stepped carefully among the vanished traces
Of nearly a hundred prostitutes from Shikoku and Kyushu,
The song
Like footprints.

Nowadays, the guides
A song that I dared not sing
Out of nowhere
Like I can hear them
in layered voices —
♪   The water that dissolves the crimson of the Shimotsui girls' makeup
Flowed out to the sea and dyed the sea bream red

The polished corridors,
Dark *shoji* screens,
The wave-beaten ceiling
Skinny words
arms
pillow
saké cup

A dark mirror stand
Spilling light to the outside
The sound of waves,
The night,
Piling ever deeper

Only words that can be spoken remain,
The unspeakable memories
Are not collected in lyrics,
They are swept away by the waves
Have you buried your bones somewhere
around here?

Or did the footprints I could never give voice
Drift away to another town?
Even now
They endure in the winds of that distant sea

The Shoe

Fingerprints on the glass door
Shimmering in the light
To rephrase in a way,
"No, it's not."
Those words…
As though somehow contaminated,
At the end of the day that was somehow off,
On flooring with no place to turn,
With an indelible aftertaste,
My aimless steps

Meeting no one face-to-face,
Days that run merely on sweet-smelling conversations
This whole town's like that,
Seasonal winds
Expose it to the cold
You could say it's like
Unwanted deference, intrusive care

Or as though letting
Your messages show as READ
Is to simultaneously fear
Connection and
Disconnection —
It's that breed of cowardice
Carrying such timidity around,
Conversations on topics that help us avoid touching each other
Are
Piled up like slippers
In the living room.

Once upon a time
When I still knew so many words
You
And I
Spoke about something,
We should have been a part of something.
But in the end, we
Simply came to understand
That would solve precisely nothing

Leaving it all behind
I put down my new shoes again,
New conversations,
New "fun things"
To seal this world's cracks.
I can't stop thinking about going somewhere
Far away

To some other place, anywhere that's not here,
To the all-severing suburbs,
The city at night,
Cruising to the end of the service road, trucks coming and going

We passed through streets lined with
cookie-cutter apartment buildings and shopping malls,
The sea breeze bent like a wire,
I carry it on my back
And run,
Running all the way through,
I arrive at
Our birthplace, on reclaimed land,
Facing the sea,
So high that we look up,
Standing in front of the concrete seawall
So high that we can't crawl up it,
We've come this far,
Yet…

In trying to protect something trivial,
I become a grain of nightscape
In a town full of thin-skinned adults
Until I wear out my thin-soled shoes
Slowly, slowly, slowly

On the sandy asphalt
Again
I get lost in the sand

Breakfast

Today, breakfast is
In the deepest part of this forest
Toast and
Scrambled eggs,
Perhaps some after-dinner coffee in a white cup?
But each bite and sip
Seems both to fill the stomach yet leave it empty

Greedy looks on our faces:
We've been suffering for so long
From a heavy constipation,
That's got us feeling blocked

Yesterday brought new dialogue
The table laid neatly with heaven,
A game of misery-seeking in support of our good fortune,
— Yet…

And when we get tired of that, what shall we do next?
You say

Leaving the TV on all through the night,
What are you staring at with such intensity
Like raking your fingernails so hard they peel off?

In that screen that I can't escape,
Somewhere far away
Across the ocean
Like something gradually dying out,
Wearing frumpy slippers
Leaving a trail of greasy fingerprints across the glassy curiosity,

That kind of
Faintly dark happiness, I want to embrace it,
We are here

In other words, it's been like
A game of fighting to steal each other's dessert
After our empty stomachs already stuffed

From a perfect posture,
We faced the food in front of us,
And made a mad dash for the dish we wanted
But when we got to it,
We could no longer remember what it was we wanted to eat.
You, me…
Stuck in this stalemate

I don't know how long it's been since I've had a morning
With such a clean and refreshing bowel movement
Like squeezing out mayonnaise —
In this small dining room,
Perhaps our world
Has long since come to a standstill,
Yet…

In the room heading for winter,
I light a fire in the stove,
This life,
Or wrapped in this template we call *Life*,
Before we grow old one day,
We go into the depths of the forest
We eat together,
Sipping tea,
And in that forest, we touch each other's ancient wounds
One more time,
I just want to spend one more night

Skin

The frontline
Is on my skin
As the site where the claw marks are cleaned away,
The site for storing away the sensations that have passed,
That is
A morning smeared with words,
The memory of a quarrel at mealtime
And the scent of a bouquet of excuses,
In sum,
I wanted to become a woman with a scar on her arm
The sound of slippers flopping is not enough
To measure the depth of this world
So I'm not a whit afraid of walking the edge of the line,
You say

In this town that will grow old before we do,
A warm, rich future
As we see that future off, as it fades into the distance,
The life that's soaked into my skin
Doesn't dry up as fast as we thought, so
It remains fresh

When I grow old, I hope my skin stays fresh,
I'm willing to lose everything for that,
I just…
I hope that
I can find a way to keep from noticing my own poverty
And that
You and I
Stay close to each other
Exchanging light words

Over our shoulders to each other,
Even though our lifestyle is not so heavy that it will ever make us can slip and fall
Crawling around on the ground —
There was no rawness to it

In other words,
Our limbo abyss
Lay on the same plane as us
In the four o'clock afternoon sunshine,
Covered in an unwashable something,
Like grains of sound spilling from headphones,
We who have grown old with our naiveté intact,
Before we know it
The distance remaining
Between the bottom of my slippers where I stepped on our spilled food
And the point we descend into our freshly desiccated old age
Is so tiny

Soon
The rain of dusk will fall

In my own intolerance
I was
Trying to acquire a plumpness to the touch

If it were possible,
I'd have wanted it to end without asking anything
If you burn away all the colors,
At the end of the afternoon with nothing but white sand and burn marks,
Like the last scene of a porno movie,
There's nothing beyond this
To the end of my skin —
Do I have to walk to the very end of my skin?

On the Road

A sleepless night –
Well, not exactly…
Just a night I didn't sleep –

In its faint light
Mingling with the atmosphere, I
Listened
To the city sounds approaching through the night
In the light sneaking in through the window,
Slipping in past the flickering curtains,
I dreamed of jumping
Off the dusty balcony
I spewed out untouchable excuses,
Some bad memory,
But, what should I have done differently?

Barefoot, I walked a short way through the night streets,
I turned to look back – no, without looking back –
As the sirens of an ambulance passed
I climbed the stairs, each step chilling the soles of my feet,
Ascending the footbridge in the dark

Somewhere,
The arrival of morning, the warmth of a plump body
Or
Someone waiting for a savior
At such a high altitude in this dim city,
Without making a sound
The flashing lights of an airplane
Glide slowly by
Maybe it was our own way
Of coming to terms with each other

When I softly close my eyes,
The light blurs in, tracing over like a finger,
The world spins
Ever so slowly,
Then describes an arc as it falls to the ground
That world is, after all,
Actually me, or so I feel

In the beginning,
I went on constantly thinking up excuses,
As though I knew they wouldn't work
Or
As though from the start, I had hoped they would fail
The people of this city
And countless machines

If there was ever a moment when all of them would stop moving
At just that moment, I would take aim and shoot this city
And then straight away,
I would fall into the soft street

It will come soon –
Sometime before the dawn

MICHIYAMA RAIN
tr. Jordan A. Y. Smith

The Memory of Light, the Memory of Water

Light falls,
Leaps off the water in response

The memory of water
Is your memory

When you looked at the water
and nodded assent,
Everything around
fled post-haste

Full of holes,
that hand
trying to capture the minute particles

The gaps vanished from
all things material and abstract
as they transformed into carpets

Get a firm grip on the rails
and there's nothing to fear,
but beyond that, there's nothing
we simply penetrate
a layer of rock thousands of times older
than the Neolithic period,
on a day called today
a marvel of day that never should have been,
making aimless detours
in our thirst for beautiful waters.

Fusion impossible –
What a dilemma –
the circumstances of an abnormal world,
my personal circumstances:
flippant
projections, nothing more

I wish things would change
I wish things would change, I think as
my unchanging self
is faithfully projected onto the world

light and
water

This moment right now
becomes engraved in their memory,
and thus we sway,
back and forth easily,
together with the Poverty of Imagination

I worry –
I worry –
All this beautiful light
in a single day –
it must be in violation of some rule,
So if breath held,
it will fall gradually into sickness

Ahh – if the earth will exist again today

buried in the strata below
transformed into rock
after thousands of centuries
excavated by a few true earth citizens
whom it greets as though to say – *Hello*.

That of all things
is not to be forgotten
is forgotten
becomes memory
in the water
filling and drying out
in the darkness
Even if I drown –
even still – somewhere
the light follows me around
it will not let me be

But no,
like reveling in the past –
this storytelling:
        your breathing

memory of light –
memory of water –
somewhere –
someone –
chit-chatting away

On a thief's mattress
sleeping peacefully –
while about the dozing crown
lurks an ethereal memory.

My First Boss

As soon as I joined the company, I joined the branch in Osaka.
My boss was old school, though that's becoming less popular –
"Hey there, Michiyama!" he says, and I reply, "Yessir!"

We were stuck in meeting rooms late every night.
We'd watch start with the evening games of his favorite baseball team,
And the night would end when he said it did.
That's just how he was, but when we would drink together, he never let me make drinks.
He'd always mix drinks for us.
He did it so often, I thought it was just a given
That bosses make drinks for younger employees.
He'd pour whisky, add soda water, mix it lightly.
"Highballs shouldn't be stirred too much.
The trick is to give them one stir, to mix top and bottom,"
He gleefully taught me.

Just once, he got terribly upset at me.
It was on a company trip to a hot spring resort,
And we were partying at the third stop of the night,
When I'd run off and fallen asleep in my bed. He came looking.
When he found me, he yelled, "At least let us know before you leave!
People will worry about you!!" and I froze up.
As time passed, I came to remember those words with joy.
After a few years, I was moved to the Tokyo office.

*

One cold winter day, the rumor reached me
That he was suddenly quitting our company.
There would be a quiet going-away party for him.
I canceled all my appointments and rushed off to catch the train.

"Hey there, you made it!"
And for the first time ever, I mixed him a highball.
"Uh, sir, just one thing…" I said.
He asked, "What it is?"
"At least let us know before you leave!
People will worry about you!!"

He paused, raised his drink, and said,
"Nice one!"

Beer

One cold winter's evening,
Just after the shop closed, a delivery order came in
As my mother helped my father load the beer crates on the back of the motorbike,
she remarked sympathetically, "Ooh, it's so cold!"
Father reassured, laughing, "Well, it's far from freezing!"
and he drove off through the dark, purplish mist.
Mother worried aloud to me, "Aw, your poor father!"
"Well, it is far from freezing!"
"But look at you, you must be so cold," she replied,
her tears catching me by surprise.

Once as I returned from a delivery in the car with my father,
I heard him repeating under his breath, "Thank you so much!" as he drove.
"Dad, are you talking?"
"Naw, I ain't talking."
Though my father tried to play it off,
I thought to myself, *He was definitely saying something…*

After I started high school,
I'd load the beer up on the motorbike
and I too would make deliveries all over town
When I'd hand people their change,
I grew so embarrassed.
After finally managing to calculate correctly,
I'd intone, *Thank you so much!*

On the way home, I'd often ponder,
And came to understand why on that day
my father had mumbled to himself, *Thank you so much!*
That was the day
I'd gotten into the University of Tokyo

Years later,
what brought me back from Tokyo
was the news of my father's heart attack

…Twenty-five years have passed since then.
I'm nearly the age he was then .
I pour him a glass of beer from the bottle,
and tell him the story.

"Father,
That winter day, when we did that delivery after the shop closed,
Was the cold really no big deal?"
As though to hide his embarrassment,
my father chugged down his beer –
Guuuuuulp!
"…Of course it was no big deal!
For you all, nothing would
be a big deal.
…Because I loved you all. "

My father was quick to get shy about things like this,
and in all his life, it was the only time he used such words.
But I understood.
I definitely understood.
When I come out of my reverie,
the young man who has come to deliver beer to me,
is standing in our entryway, shyly saying,

  Thank you so much!

Without a doubt, the young man is my father,
and he is also me.

YOTSUMOTO YASUHIRO

Japanese Poetry:

Where did we come from, what are we, and where will we go?

THE TOSA DIARY AS A CONTEMPORARY JAPANESE POEM

I understand that T. S. Eliot once said something to the effect of, if you want to be a poet even after the age of twenty-five, a sense of history is almost indispensable.[1] Really? If so, I must have failed to be one. It never occurred to me, until recently, that you need any historical context for writing poetry. I always believed that poetry, unlike an academic paper or a new law, be generated directly out of the "here & now," without any before or after. A flower in a vast wasteland.

Yet, over the years, I have gradually become aware of the continuity in the tradition of writing poetry from the ancient *Manyoushu* via renga and haiku in the ages leading up to the innovation of *shintaishi* (new-style, free-form) poems in Meiji era all the way to this "here & now" in the twenty-first century. The realization came to me not so much intellectually, but rather intuitively as I kept writing and reading. All the past poets, whom I used to consider either irrelevant or something you must fight against and break away from, now seem more like your fellow colleagues. I know, I'm getting old.

Let's take Ki no Tsurayuki, who edited the *Kokinwakashu*, the first royal anthology, in 905 as an emerging waka poet. Then he wrote *The Tosa Diary*, a combination of prose and verses based on his boat trip from Tosa (today's Kochi) back to Kyoto after completing a five-year assignment as a local governor. I now find this work of his, which is no more than one hundred paperback pages, as relevant and exciting as any contemporary poems written today in Japan.

As many of you know, the opening sentence of this book goes, "Let me try this diary thing, which is a man's thing to do." Tsurayuki the author pretends to be a servant woman, making a journal during the 55-day boat trip with her master Tsurayuki as a main character. Note that he is swapping not only the gender, but also the social and cultural implications that go with it. Those include, first and foremost, the ownership of languages and the designated domain of poetry between men and women.

---

1 From Eliot's "Tradition and the Individual Talent," "[…] the historical sense, which we may call nearly indispensable to anyone who would continue to be a poet beyond his twenty-fifth year […]."

Prior to the Tsurayuki's era, the official court language was Chinese, which was monopolized by men. Women were expected to only speak Japanese and the writing system of kana was just being developed. This had a direct influence on the sociology of poetry: only men could compose, read and recite Chinese style poems (漢詩 kanshi), which were considered to be superior to the indigenous Japanese poetry form, waka, literally meaning Japanese (和) song (歌). In fact, waka were considered to be occasional and private poems mostly for building romantic relationships between men and women. Kanshi were essentially written language poetry for Japanese men, although they were often recited aloud as well. You had to learn the Chinese language by reading and writing to start with. On the other hand, waka had a long history of being a spoken language poetry without an adequate writing system.

Tsurayuki obviously tried to break up this hierarchy and create something totally new through the crash and integration of those opposing elements: men—women, master—servant, the Chinese language (poetry)—the Japanese language (poetry), writing—speaking, letters—voices, and prose—verse. A poetry-diary made by a woman servant was a perfect vehicle to realize this ambitious attempt.

Before the voyage started, the servant woman made an entry about a farewell party held for her master Tsurayuki. She saw the men get drunk and start to recite Chinese poems: "Well, I can't write them down because I don't know the Chinese characters. But wait! My master just recited a waka that went……" This shows that Tsurayuki the author was fully aware of the social and cultural gap in the community where Tsurayuki the real man was in the leadership position.

Later in the diary, the woman narrator recalled Abe no Nakamaro, an eighth-century man who was sent to Tang-dynasty China as a Japanese envoy and spent more than 50 years in this foreign land. At one point, he tried to go home and the local people held a farewell party for him (just like the Tosa people did for her departing master). She recounted a waka composed by Nakamaro for the occasion, which goes something like: "There rises the moon over the blue ocean. I wonder if that is the same moon I used to see over the mountain in my hometown." Then she made a remark, which can be roughly translated as follows:

> Sure the Chinese people don't understand Nakamaro's waka written in Japanese. But if you use the men's characters (meaning Chinese characters), they should get some idea about what he was singing about. Further, if you ask a Chinese person who understands our language (meaning Japanese) to translate it, they would even be impressed! Even though the languages are different between the two countries, the moon in the sky is the same. So should be a human heart: we can communicate and share the same emotion despite the language barrier.

Isn't this amazing? This is all about the translation of literature and you wouldn't expect to hear it from the mouth of a servant woman narrator created a thousand years ago. It struck me as one of the clearest testimonies for the continuity from the past to the present in the history of Japanese poetry, because the dualities of the Chinese language and the indigenous Japanese language persist till today and affect our poetry writing in a profound way.

KANSHI AND WAKA AS DNA OF CONTEMPORARY JAPANESE POETRY

You might have been puzzled to read what I just wrote. Are Chinese style poems (kanshi) still relevant today? Who is reading them? I myself would have said no 10 years ago, before I tried to translate some classic Tang-dynasty poems, mainly Li Bai's and Du Fu's, in such a manner that the translated texts could pass as contemporary Japanese poems. The experience helped me realize this surprising truth: the logical and conceptual elements of Japanese poetry owe a lot to the heritage of writing and reading Chinese style poems. It was surprising because I had long thought that it had rather been Western poetry, which came to Japan only after it opened its door to the outside world in the mid-nineteenth century, that had been the biggest influence.

It is certainly true that the introduction of Western poetry, especially poems from the English romanticist and French symbolist traditions, had an enormous impact on the development of the so-called *kōgojiyū-shi* (口語自由詩, spoken-language, free-form poems), which we all practice today including yours truly. The novel concepts of Freedom, Love, and Individuality, and the way those concepts were expressed in Western poetry shocked Japanese poets and they strived for mastering their own way of doing the same in Japanese. But it was the long heritage of Chinese-style poetry which enabled them to accept and digest Western poetry. This heritage taught Japanese poets, over more than fourteen centuries, how to read and write poems in a foreign language which is more logical and structured than their own. If it were not for this collective training, the Meiji poets would have had a tougher time dealing with their Western counterparts.

Ōoka Makoto, one of the most influential poets and critics of our time, wrote extensively about the rivalry between kanshi and waka in the Heian era. He considered Sugawara Michizane (845-903) as the best kanshi poet, whereas the younger Kino Tsurayuki was regarded as the flag bearer of waka form, which took over the position of the official poetry of Japan from kanshi. Oooka also wrote that, before the Meiji era, when you said "poetry" (*shi* 詩), it only meant kanshi. Waka was instead called "song" (*uta* 歌).

Just recently, I also found that Kido Shuri, a poet and critic of the same age as I, had written more than twenty years ago about the significant role of Chinese-style poetry for the development of modern Japanese poetry. He pointed out that many free-form poems were written in the late Edo era, long before the introduction of the Western poetry, and attributed them to the tradition of kanshi.

Now that I have learned about this history, it is almost impossible not to become aware of the kanshi elements engineered into my own writing, along with those of waka, renga and haiku, like DNA. I tend to get closer to the former when I write poems dealing with social and political issues, and to the latter when I write more personal and lyrical poems. Can I somehow combine the two streams to create something new? Then I realized that that was precisely what Ki no Tsurayuki did by writing *The Tosa Diary* eleven centuries ago.

A SHORT READING LIST

So this is where we are from—at least one aspect of it. But where are we now? I have to say that I am the least qualified person to provide a comprehensive sketch of the landscape of Japanese poetry today, as I just came back to the country last spring after a 34-year absence. So it would be more like a first impression from an outsider.

One thing that struck me was the large number of new poetry books that are sent to me. I used to receive a few even when I was in Germany, but now I'm back in Japan it has become literally overwhelming,and I now live under the imminent danger of a book avalanche. Then I started teaching poetics in some universities. It's not a creative writing course, but I was amazed by the large number of students who voluntarily submit their poems each week. It seems like there is a great appetite, or even an urge, among the Japanese, young and old, men and women, to write poems, if not to read them. Is it a good thing? I guess so for the industry, but it may also be an indication of anxiety and loneliness rooted in our society. Poetry thrives under adversity, especially of the spiritual kind.

Another thing I noticed was that most of those poems were the accounts of the authors' inner world. They are personal and emotive, uttered in whispered voices and written with sophisticated techniques. In other words, they are closer to the tradition of waka as opposed to kanshi, in that they tend to lack self-assertion and a larger, social perspective. The overall impression is that we now live in the New Heian period, when waka replaced kanshi as the official poetry form for the nation. (This impression is further reinforced by the fact that most students in my classes are so shy and quiet that you think they are absent-minded, only to find out later after reading their "*Ria-pe*" (reaction paper) that each buries under a façade a deep and rich private world.)

But there are some poets who go beyond personal territory and bravely tackle the larger issues in social, cultural, or political arenas. The following are just a few of those poets who struck me as twenty-first century versions of Kino Tsurayuki, and who try to combine both elements of the waka and kanshi:

Tokisato Jiro: His most recent collection *Naijima Island* (『名井島』思潮社 2018) blew my mind by presenting an epic saga of artificial intelligence seeking the secrets of the human language, long after the annihilation of our civilization. It is the telling of an SF story, criticism of human consciousness and language, and a lyric poem all at once. If you have not read it yet, do it now. If you are tempted to translate it into English, let me know. I will join you.

Arai Takako: Born as a daughter of a family running a textile factory in Kiryu, the place long known for its silk production, Takako made a vivid account of the lives of the female factory workers in her earlier works, such as *Factory Girls* (Action Books 2019). It is a poetic documentary (an insider report) about post-war Japan, which enjoyed the miraculous economic growth made only possible by the hard work of those women. The use of the local dialect in the dramatic monologue is outstanding in Japanese poetry, which is almost always written in standard Japanese.

Her most recent book, *The Songs of Ishikawa Takuboku, in the Tohoku Old Women's Dialect* (『東北おんば訳　石川啄木のうた』 未来社 2017) brought this exploration into the possibility of using local dialects into a new dimension. Takako met those women (called "onba" in Northeastern Japan) in the temporary housing units set up after the 3.11 earthquake, and started a series of workshops with those onba to translate the tanka of Ishikawa Takuboku into their own words. The result is a magical rebirth of the household classic tanka through the rubble of the monstrous disaster.

Park Kyongmi: Kyongmi is a Japanese language poet with Korean family roots. Her father, who smuggled himself to Japan in the wake of the Jeju Island April 3 uprising in 1948 as a dissident student, is now old and declining, away from his home country. *Let go by yourself* (『ひとりで行け』 栗売社 2021) is the title of her latest collection. It is an elegy to her father who went by himself to Japan as a young man and is now getting ready to go to the other world, leaving his loved ones behind on both occasions. Through this juxtaposition, Kyongmi creates a poetic trinity of man, history, and eternity. You can read her earlier works in English translation in *Four from Japan: Contemporary Poetry & Essays by Women* (translated by Sawako Nakayasu and Cole Swensen, Litmus Press 2006)

Osaki Sayaka: Sayaka made her debut as a poet in 2011, the devastating year of the earthquake, tsunami, and nuclear meltdown. It is not a coincidence that the narrator of her works is often 'we', rather than 'I', sharing the sense of community to which you, the reader, also belong. Her latest collection *Freedom to Dance* (『踊る自由』左右社 2021), just published this summer, leads us further into the maze of the psychological underground of our society, but there is something refreshingly new about it. Is it hope? Or the will for freedom?

THE FUTURE IN THE WIND

Finally, we have reached the third question: where are we going? The answer, my friend, is blowin' in the wind. The answer is blowin' in the wind. But one thing is certain. We have been writing poems for more than 1400 years, and reciting them even longer, constantly stretching the edges of the poem and coming up with new forms and styles. We are doomed to continue that tradition and I am happy to be a part of it.

Fall 2021

STEPHEN SNYDER

Talks Translation

In April 2021, renowned translator and Dean of Language Schools and Kawashima Professor of Japanese Studies at Middlebury College in Vermont, Stephen Snyder joined ToPoJo Editors Barbara Summerhawk, Jeffrey Johnson, and Jordan A. Y. Smith for a video conversation on literary translation.

We've all been fans of his translations into English for decades of Ogawa Yoko, Ōe Kenzaburō, Kirino Natsuo, Murakami Ryu, Yu Miri, and Nagai Kafu and others. Though not a poetry translator per se, there is poetry in every line Snyder touches, and we joyfully seized the chance to siphon off his font of linguistic and cultural wisdom.

BARBARA SUMMERHAWK

I'd like you to meet colleagues of mine, Jordan Smith, who is an extraordinary translation professor at Josai International University, a poet and a linchpin in our operation, as well as Jeffrey Johnson, professor at Daito, a poet and poetry translator. I'm not a translator, I'm a dilettante, notoriously unreliable in technological things; and Stephen Snyder, of course, you all are familiar with. Did you get the questions?

STEPHEN SNYDER

I did, and I just want to say: Hi, it's so nice to meet both of you! And if the questions are yours, Jordan, it is the best set of questions I have ever read. So thank you very much. I can't do justice to a number of them. But they were super fun to think about.

BARBARA

It's a mix of questions from all of us. This first one is Jordan's question, and Jordan can ask it.

JORDAN A. Y. SMITH

We know some people think literary translation is this incredibly complex matrix of linguistic knowledge and literary craft awash in the politics of global publishing and transnational stereotypes, one that can only be navigated with the utmost care. But, could you just tell us how to do it in say, fifty words or less?

STEPHEN

I'm hoping this will be a conversation partly because I know that all three of you have incredible knowledge about this field, and partly because *TPJ* is a poetry journal—and, right now, I have to say that I have no experience with poetry. I have translated a few poems, and a few song lyrics only on the occasion of having them embedded in a narrative. And otherwise, I don't take on poetry, and for reasons I'm happy to talk about.

I think translation has suddenly become a really interesting kind of minefield of politics in (maybe) a wonderful way, an interesting way… I've been talking with friends particularly about the Amanda Gorman controversy. [Her would-be Dutch translator (a novelist who won the International Booker in 2020) withdrew from the project after a number of complaints that suggested a translator who shared identity with Gorman would be more appropriate. The discussion about who should or should not translate particular texts in the wake of this has been compelling.] "Controversy" isn't the right word. It's such a fascinating topic, not only about who can translate, a bit about what the field looks like, but in my own case, I'll just limit it to my experience and say that for me, translation—this is way more than fifty words already—but for me, translation is always a negotiation. It's sentence by sentence, lexical item by lexical item. It's an attempt to balance the pressures of, obviously, the author's need and my need to make the author's language literal, and to make it readable for the reader. So every sentence on every page is a negotiation between those two values.

BARBARA

I'd like to go on with that for a minute—something you said at Daito when you came to speak to the graduate students. When you were translating *Coin Locker Babies* [by Murakami Ryu], the publisher asked you to take out an entire chapter. And, that's a negotiation—but that wasn't a negotiation, was it? It was a kind of command from the publisher, or literally from the editor.

STEPHEN

It was a command from the editor. The negotiation actually was with Ryu himself. So interestingly, the editor said, the book is too long. This particular chapter doesn't fit. If you know the book, it's a kind of double helix plot that alternates chapters between the two coin locker babies. This particular chapter was, he felt, extremely gratuitous to the double helix rhythm, so he told me that he wanted to take it out. He said, "Would you call Ryu and ask him to take it out?" So the negotiation was on a phone conversation with Ryu, who is an incredibly generous man and has been very good to me over the years, and is a very interesting person to talk to. He was unenthusiastic about this suggestion when I talked to him on the phone, but ultimately, he agreed with the editor, and it is a chapter that is not included in the English translation.

BARBARA

Did that affect the translation? Was that chapter an important chapter?

STEPHEN

No, it doesn't advance the plot at all and that's the reason that the editor wanted it deleted, he felt it was sort of meandering. It is a very plot-driven book, and it was a moment when it should have been moving forward, but it failed to do so because of that chapter. But in retrospect, it's a decision I somewhat regret. And that's the negotiation piece. I would have had to push back against the editor. But this was the second book I ever translated. I was many, many years younger, it is the only book I ever translated that I had selected and offered to an editor. It was something I was very anxious to do, and I didn't feel like I was in the position to push back that hard on the editor, but it doesn't damage the novel tremendously.

JORDAN

I'd just like to offer *Tokyo Poetry Journal* as a venue for publishing that unpublished chapter and we can add line breaks and make it read like a poem, and poems are known for not necessarily advancing plots, so it may just have a second home.

STEPHEN

It would be fascinating, wouldn't it? I would be curious to ask Ryu whether after all these years he'd like to see it in print and *Tokyo Poetry Journal* would be the ideal venue, I agree.

BARBARA

And we would need to take liberties to put it into a poetic form.

STEPHEN

Right, actually, I won't describe it now. The only time it's really come up is when Sean Lennon actually optioned the film rights to make *Coin Locker Babies* into a movie. And the person he hired—now I can't remember the man's name—but the person he hired to do the screenplay got in touch with me, now this was years later, to ask if he could see that chapter because he wanted to know if it should be in a film version. It's a very visual chapter and it might have been interesting, but the film never happened. I'm sure it would have been a really interesting film, more interesting anime actually.

JORDAN

Cool idea. You were mentioning, with translation, that it's this kind of lexical negotiation, and that in general, you stick more with prose fiction, rather than with poetry, although, prose fiction sometimes brings you into the territory of poetry by quoting or having a poem inside of a text. What are your reasons for sticking with prose? More just personal preference? Or is there something about the translation of poetry that has made that seem like not your cup of tea? Or how did that play out?

STEPHEN

I see it as a limitation in my abilities. I feel as though I never had an ambition to be a writer or a short story writer, although I think every translator secretly has that somewhere, but I absolutely love the process of converting Japanese prose into English prose. And, I feel like it's something about which after many, many years of doing this, I have a certain facility, but poetry because of all the cliches—the inability to separate the meaning from the sound, from the words, the ways in which it defeats any attempt to be literal in between English and Japanese—is something that every time I look at, I just can't imagine how I would approach it.

I teach a translation seminar, and I have the students translate poetry at the beginning before they start their prose, and almost all of them end up translating prose for their semester project. But the first few days we translate poetry because I want them to see that difficulty, kind of impenetrability, the incommensurability, between Japanese and English, that for me, is so much more evident with poetry, and I weep when I think what poets have to go through. But I also believe deeply that someone who translates poetry needs to be a poet and I'm not a poet.

JORDAN

Do you have set poets that you choose for the students to work on? Or do you ask students to go out and find poets?

STEPHEN

At this level, it's something I provide them with, and I have a number of exercises around poetry—it's all tanka, I haven't even ventured into modern poetry. It's all tanka and waka, or haiku and so it's kind of canned. It would be interesting to have them try something that's more modern, but I've never gone that route.

JORDAN

I think tanka is definitely one of the more mind-blowingly difficult forms to translate. We did a workshop once where we had three translators including Eric Selland and Andy Houwen, and myself, and then three tanka poets. They each contributed three tanka poems, and then we all prepared three different translations and then we all got together and had a big workshop discussion and there was absolutely zero agreement on anything at any stage.

BARBARA

That was the one we did at Infinity Books—Tanka and Translation. In Volume 9, Watanabe Mieko, a lesbian poet who has written a lot of lesbian-based poetry, had written some tanka that she wanted translated. Laurie Walters was trying to translate the tanka, but it was almost impossible. The metaphors she was using, the tanka form itself—it was all so difficult. I got back to the author that the tanka was proving too daunting for our experienced, but volunteer, translator. The author rolled with it; she was disappointed, but I couldn't ask the translator to donate her time to spend hours more with that difficult task.

STEPHEN

It's daunting, it really is. And I do the same kind of exercise, I give a couple of tanka and have all, whatever it is, six or ten students in the class each do a translation. And as you say, Jordan, they're all completely different. There's no sort of overlap in the approach they take, which is part of the fascination, but it does leave me kind of exhausted to think about.

I worked at the University of Colorado Boulder for fifteen years, and Laurel Rodd, who has translated both the *Kokinshu* and the *Shin-Kokinshu*, is a dear friend, as is Stephen Miller, who has worked on Buddhist poetry from the Imperial collections, for all their careers, and they do brilliant translations, but the things they have to do to make it an academic exercise, as well as a poetic exercise, to make sense of the whole range of reference in the vocabulary, and to understand the particular court situation, was more than I can deal with. Andy Houwen, and myself, and then three tanka poets. They each contributed three tanka poems, and then we all prepared three different translations and then we all got together and had a big workshop discussion and there was absolutely zero agreement on anything at any stage.

JORDAN

This makes me think back to you saying translation is always a negotiation. And so it sounds like you just don't negotiate with terrorists.

STEPHEN

Exactly right. And tanka poets are terrorists when it comes to… [laughter]

JEFFREY JOHNSON

What strategies have you seen students come up with to preserve the cultural and linguistic uniqueness in the original work?

STEPHEN

What's changed over time in the thirty-plus years that I've been doing this? I would say that my students consistently have decided that when they're doing their translations, they can leave many more terms and concepts in the original than was ever permissible or possible thirty years ago.

So a fairly esoteric food term can come up, and they're perfectly willing to leave it in Japanese. Their assumption is that, in their own world, they were going to Japanese restaurants, and everybody knows what, let's say "gari"—the sushi term for ginger— is. If nobody does know it, people will Google it, and they'll understand immediately. I've seen this actually beyond Japanese fiction, and I've seen it very frequently now in other translations as well, where people just leave words or whole passages in the original language, and the assumption is that people will figure out what they mean or can Google them. That has changed radically.

When I started, I couldn't use the word "tofu," I had to use bean curd. And Linda [Stephen's wife] was just telling me, I haven't reread the translation of Kirino Natsuo's *Out*, for many, many years, but she teaches it pretty regularly, and she was telling me that in that whole translation, they never use the word "bento" even though it's all centered around a bento factory in western Tokyo. But they use the word lunchbox throughout the whole novel, and of course, everyone in America knows what a bento is. There's kind of an absurdist quality if the translation sounds very dated when you read it. Now, fortunately, I don't have to go back and read it. But that's the type of thing that has changed, you know, very rapidly for the better, this ability.

I may have mentioned that I'm chairing the judging panel for the National Book Award for translated fiction this year, and just got asked to do that. And it involves reading 130 novels in the next two months. So it's not really a good idea—but it's super fun! I was just reading a novel that's translated from Arabic, but there is a lot of Arabic, even Arabic script, just left in the text. So I don't know if you're familiar with Mizumura Minae's *Shishosetsu from Left to Right*, it's just been translated and published by Columbia. But originally, the novel had large passages of English just interspersed with the Japanese because it was describing the kind of bilingual worlds she grew up in. But she was prescient in the sense that now lots of people are doing the same kind of thing, even translators are doing it.

JORDAN

It was the novel that she predicted could be translated into any language except English, I believe.

STEPHEN

Yeah, it loses all meaning because the inner text you know, between the Japanese and English, disappears if you translate everything into English.

JORDAN

So there's no way to get that back and forth. All of that brings up the super interesting question of untranslatability. I worked on a funky book with Yoshimizu Gōzō (Forrest Gander's editorial and translatorly creation, *Alice Iris Red Horse*), and with that forefront in mind, how do you deal with experimental, unruly material? What do you do with texts that push translation to the limits or that call for radical moves or wild and wily, creative translation tactics? And I just wonder if, in your experience with translation, if you ever pulled some crazy thing that you're particularly proud of and wanted to signal? Or if you've ever seen another translator employ an innovative method that makes you pause, whether in shock or awe.

STEPHEN

It's such a good question. And if I were better organized or smarter, I would be collecting these examples. Every time I come across a passage and think, oh, that's pretty hot, I should just write it down in some notebook and keep them all because I do get asked this question from time to time.

A move that someone else made that has impressed me for years—I've talked about this before but will here again because I think it's a foundational one for the translation of Japanese prose anyway—is Alfred Birnbaum's translation of *Hitsuji wo meguru boken* (*A Wild Sheep Chase*), and I think even the title, which is just a brilliant transition into something so so clever in English, and so vernacular, that's indicative of everything he does in that translation. I admire and am good friends with Phil Gabriel, and Jay Rubin is my *senpai*. I think they've both done extraordinary work, but I love Alfred's early translations. I think he sets the tone for the way Murakami is going to be in English. And *A Wild Sheep Chase* is really the place he does that.

And if you know the passage toward the end—this is a famous incident in translation studies—I think, but the sheepman who's the character, in the Japanese, it simply says he speaks very quickly. But what Alfred did, and here I think he was also collaborating with the editor, Elmer Luke, they decided to close up all the spaces between all the words in the dialogue that the sheepman speaks. It's not an effect that exists in Japanese because there are no word spaces in Japanese, but it's tremendously impressive on the page. And it becomes a kind of visual joke of the novel, but it's completely a creation, an epiphenomenon of the translation and their cleverness. There are so many examples throughout that translation and others by Alfred that I think we all would aspire to.

I'll tell you one example that I've also mentioned elsewhere that is purely serendipity, when I was translating Ogawa's *Hakase no aishita sushiki* (*The Housekeeper and the Professor*), there's a passage there where the professor is helping a little boy do his homework and the homework consists of coming up with palindromes and of course, palindromes are, by definition, completely untranslatable. (Incidentally, Murakami has a fascinating book of palindromes, Japanese palindromes, that is one of the few works of his that no one will ever translate.)

But for this passage, because you had to have some palindromes as examples of what they were doing in the homework, I actually worked with the editor, and we made a long list of palindromes and then just sort of substituted them in for the Japanese when it was appropriate. But the professor is a math professor, of course, and the book revolves around a lot of math material. And the final palindrome that the professor comes up with in the Japanese novel is "reitou toire" ["frozen toilet"]. You know—it's cute, it's funny, and they all laugh. It's not particularly germane to the plot. But we discovered and I give due credit to the editor here, David Rogers, but David and I were going through this list, and we realized that there's a common palindrome in English, "I prefer pi." As in, the number, the irrational number ϖ. And of course, pi is one of the central tropes of the novel. So to have just by chance, a perfect palindrome that embodies the theme of the novel, so perfectly, it's a way in which the translation then gets a kind of excellence that wasn't even possible in the original. I love to go back to that—recall the pleasure of it.

JEFFREY

That dovetails with my other question—I had a lead-in about Edgar Allan Poe being translated into French. And so I think you've given us an example of an answer right now. But could you expatiate on that a little bit? Is it possible for a translation to exceed or uncover the greatness of an original that maybe isn't quite so apparent in the original?

STEPHEN

I would put it differently. I love that question, and certainly there are examples— Yoshimoto Banana, I think, is more popular in Italy still than she is in Japan anymore, but… Well, this novel that I most recently translated was *Memory Police* (*Hisoyaka na kessho*), which is twenty-five years old in Japan. And I'd like to talk about it in terms of the afterlife, which Walter Benjamin refers to somehow, in the case of this novel, it was less about the translation and more about the serendipity of the timing. It was a novel that feels very much like a Trumpian world. And then, again, through the twelve months after the publication of the book, when the paperback came out, it was just as lockdown made it feel like we were losing things in the same way that people lose them in the novel in the memory palace. So there is a way in which translation can reposition, can repurpose, fiction that's existed for a while—in this case, for twenty-five years—and in the original cultural context, and in the new cultural context, that takes on a lot of new meaning. And that happened with that particular novel for sure. I don't think it brought out any excellences that weren't already there. It's just that the happenstance of the way it appeared in the west at that particular time was pretty fortunate.

JORDAN

Brings to mind the way that literary translation, between Japan and the U.S., is responsible for another kind of negotiation, which is that between national images, right, the way that the Anglophone-reading community perceives Japan, and the question is kind of a dual one: how does literary translation, or how has literary translation, from Japanese to English, changed that image actively over the last few decades? Or do you see images of Japan, perceptions of Japan, determining the kinds of books that get into translation?

STEPHEN

You know, since I began reading Japanese fiction a very long time ago now, the image of Japan that comes through in that fiction is absolutely altered and varied in much more interesting ways than it was. Ted [Edward] Fowler, and you probably are familiar with the articles he wrote years ago in the *Journal of Japanese Studies*, talked about the way that particular publishers, and in particular translators, really the generation of my teachers, shaped the postwar image of Japanese literature and to some extent the image of Japan through the translation of essentially Tanizaki, Kawabata, and Mishima published by New Directions and Knopf. And it really was an attempt, as Ted argues, I think brilliantly, to kind of reposition Japan after the war from being a bellicose enemy to being a Zen-focused potential ally in the Far East. And so that was, in a way that was what Japanese fiction was, and the rest of Japanese fiction again, this is Ted's argument not mine, is in many ways ignored through that period through the 50s and 60s.

And even into the 70s, humorous fiction, for instance, or mysteries or genre fiction or much of it was completely ignored. It was just this fairly narrow stripe of literary fiction by a particular kind of writer. I think what happens after that is that—and here again, I credit Alfred and others—but I think that his *Monkey Brain Sushi* volume, which began to publish and bring to attention a much broader range of contemporary writers, had a huge influence on changing the perception of Japan. And I've argued in a variety of places that it was perfectly timed with a fairly conscious attempt by Japan to begin to use its popular culture soft power, so the whole cliche of Cool Japan. They needed a kind of cultural product that would in some ways be the literary equivalent of the Sony Walkman or the Honda Civic—something that was extremely marketable.

I think Murakami ultimately became that product, and we can talk about his influence, but I think that in many ways, there was a moment there, the way Yoshimoto Banana's *Kitchen* was marketed. Even in the beginning, when Yamada Amy's first novels came out and Murakami Ryu's to a lesser extent, all of these books completely reshaped the vision of what Japan was in the eyes of the West, and it became then a kind of a symbol of the modern or even the postmodern, instead of this aestheticized postwar group.

JORDAN

The writing from Fowler that you're talking about transformed my entire way of thinking about world literature and in some ways led to this kind of direction and the questions, so I'm pleased to hear you pick that up too. And it's interesting to think of the ways that you've also intervened in that—if I remember correctly, the Japanese Literary Publishing Project, it was said to have a kind of gatekeeping function, right? Have you ever worked with them?

STEPHEN

I have worked with them non-stop. I'm actually on their payroll since the year it started, around 2002 or 2003. I was in Japan at the time when it was being formed. And actually, I was working on this endless project that will never see the light of day other than in piecemeal, but it's an ethnography of the publishing industry. I actually went and talked with the woman who was founding it, she was *amakudari* ["golden parachute" hire] from the Japan Foundation. She was given the purse strings and given the task of setting up the structure, and I interviewed her, but then basically became one of her advisors for the English piece of it, so I've worked with them constantly. I was on the selection committee for novels for about three years out of the ten or twelve years that they did it.

Most of the other times, it was a group of University of Tokyo *senseis*, and I was one of the few non-Japanese people in those years. It wasn't always a fraught project. It had really great intentions. I think it did many, many good things. But the text selection piece of it was always difficult. It was very hard for them to identify what would really succeed. I think they did wonderful things. It did morph, after about 2012, into a different entity that is still called JLPP. It sponsors the International Translation Competition, and I've served on the prize jury for every one of the prizes. So yes, my fingerprints, I'm afraid, are all over that thing. And I will say that the prize piece of it has been really valuable. They've identified several of the people who were either the runners-up or the winners and have gone on to become excellent translators and published translators. Sam Bett was one of the early winners, and of course has done an amazing job with a number of writers already. I think that actually the more effective activity than trying to identify works to translate, is to let the market and the publishing industry take care of that, and their explicit goal now is to try to raise the next generation of other effective translators.

JORDAN

It seems like Japanese literature in English is really going in a great direction over the last couple of decades. There's a much wider variety of Japanese authors and texts getting into translation. There's more than a handful now of contemporary authors that are household names, at least among lit-loving households. I wonder if we could tack on the question I believe Barbara has asked, about ways of expanding diversity. What are the strategies of broadening the path or increasing the diversity of authors and texts and translation to show the true variety of writers and literary texts coming out of Japan?

BARBARA

I saw your Berkeley presentation at the conference in which there seemed to be an understated snark involved in the presentation about Murakami Haruki. But in any case, when you came to Daito, you said that you had just come back from New York where you sat in a room with all white men deciding what novels were going to be published for the next year from the Japanese. You mentioned that the number of novels translated from English into Japanese is thirty-five, compared to one novel going the other way, and that this is true, not just for Japanese, but for Arabic and for other languages as well. You traced how Murakami was marketed and the kinds of things that went on with that. What we're trying to do is to present some poets who might not have had access to an international audience. I did the same thing with *A Sparkling Rain*. Nakayama Kaho won the Akutagawa prize, and she was desperate to get into English. She's a popular writer here in Japan, but she probably never would have been picked up because of her lesbian-based themes. I'm just curious about how we increase the diversity of judges or the people doing this kind of selection?

STEPHEN

It's a great question. That group of all white men that you were talking about was actually the first iteration of the JLPP. And then they went to a domestic selection committee, that was a one-time thing only when it was just being formed. As Jordan said earlier, I think things are moving in a great direction, partly that there's so many younger, very able translators of both prose and poetry. I mean, Jeffrey Angles is no longer a beginner, but Jeffrey has just done an amazing amount to promote the translation of Japanese poetry and Japanese poets around the world in a very visible way. But there are lots of really good, younger translators who work directly with publishers who have connections to the American publishing industry. Someone like Allison Markin Powell—she is an absolutely extraordinary translator and has done wonderful work with Kawakami Hiromi and many others. She is an advocate for expanding the pool of translators, the sort of diversity of representation of translators. I went to a Zoom talk she gave yesterday at Boston University where she presented a bunch of really interesting statistics about who translates Japanese literature and what it is they're translating, and even in the past five years, despite the fact that we have so many Japanese women writers, winning prizes, and in this moment, when Japanese women writers are perceived as a global phenomenon, she went back and looked at all the numbers, and still, it's about twice as many men who are translated into English, and that the translators are predominantly male, now that the statistics are actually getting better. Over the past five years, the number she was presenting gets close to parity in 2020. There's still a long way to go in trying to figure out how to make the pool of translators more representative, and then to try to figure out whether there are writers out there who we should be translating, whoever they are.

JORDAN

Allison's work as a translator and with Strong Women, Soft Power has surely been a huge part of any shift toward gender parity among JE translators. In terms of who gets most of the major prizes (like the Akutagawa, that B mentioned) in Japanese literature, it's fairly equal, or women authors are starting to inch into a tiny majority with some. But specifically in North American, and in general Anglophone publishing of Japanese literature, the gender imbalance is an effect of the literary translation publishing industry, though, right?

STEPHEN

Absolutely. She had those statistics as well. So the Akutagawa prize was actually won by more women than men in recent years. The prize had been slightly skewed toward men. But it was very close. In either case, I did a little bit of work looking at the French publishing industry. And of course, they're translating Japanese fiction, Japanese literature in general more regularly than anyone in the United States. I'd be interested in looking at the numbers there as well, I suspect they're skewed male in the case of French publishing.

BARBARA

I just wanted to ask a follow-up to a question that Jordan put out. If you knew that there were no gatekeepers, and you knew that you could get something published, who would you choose to translate?

STEPHEN

So, I have to admit, I haven't lived in Japan regularly for many years now, and I have a day job that prevents me from reading widely, so I'm not the best judge. I cannot keep up with the incredible onslaught of Japanese fiction. I read just basically the writers who I'm already familiar with, and there are dozens of novels literally just among those people. Ogawa Yoko has fifteen books that someone ought to translate into English. I would—and I'm hoping to do as many of them as I can before I run out of steam—but there are four or five wonderful novels by Nakagami Kenji, who I have huge admiration for. *Karekinada* (The Sea of Withered Trees), I think, particularly is an incredible masterpiece and should be translated. Someone's worked on it for quite some time in several contexts, but it's never seen the light of day in English and it certainly deserves to.

BARBARA

Nakagami Kenji is from Shingū in Wakayama, isn't he? He was a *burakumin*, and you know *Hinamatsuri* was made into a movie, which is just mind-blowing. And I've been to his birthplace there. And when I go back to Shingū to visit, and I visit some of the Aikido folks, they've all read him, and everybody knows who he is, and so forth. He really does deserve more exposure.

STEPHEN

And there were two really good collections of short stories, including Eve Zimmerman's really good collection, but the full-length novels have never been published.

JORDAN

I've got a boring question on that. It's something that we wrestle with at *Tokyo Poetry Journal*, which is the debate between print and electronic or digital publishing. And obviously, one of the most pragmatic concerns with publication and the reason that there's so much gatekeeping involved is that there's a lot of costs in mass-producing books. But that can be solved so easily with digital means, I mean, essentially, anyone who can get their translation into a decent shape, get permission, and put it out, has that opportunity. I wonder what you think about the digital publishing world? And if you see that as an answer, or if you feel that it's risky for quality control and stuff. What are your thoughts about the digital publishing world?

STEPHEN

It's such a fascinating question. And I suspect you know a lot more about it, even to be able to pose the question so eloquently. I haven't given it a lot of thought, because I've been sort of exclusively focused on the print media. But obviously, it's an amazing sort of venue for publishing virtually anything. I think that the difficulty is that you have brilliant writers whose work is dispersed in a sense, the audiences are so disaggregated and so niche that it's hard to gain the kind of reputation that the print media or print books can garner for somebody. So I'm not absolutely sure.

And it may be a generational thing, because obviously, reputation on Instagram and Facebook has wider recognition now than reading a review in the *New York Times* will get you. So it's possible that is the way that reading will go. I went to another talk yesterday, two talks yesterday by a former student of mine who's working on a dissertation at the University of Washington, and she's working on Twitter novels, and the relationship between readers and writers of Twitter novels.

And I know that there were text novels—I think text novels in Japan were briefly, and maybe still are extraordinarily popular, and they were even then being printed as paper editions.

So there's clearly a porous boundary between these two things, and there's a world out there, but it's not one that I'm familiar enough with to comment on whether that's going to be a way to disseminate what at this point is considered literary fiction or serious poetry. But I'd love to know what you all think. Is there, for instance, a vibrant world of online poetry publication? I mean, this is beautiful, *Tokyo Poetry Journal*, absolutely beautiful. And I think it's important to have the paper form.

JEFFREY

That's in our manifesto.

BARBARA

When Jeffrey and I sat down to start this thing, we were always going to have a print volume. When you put things online, people stop looking at it. That's my impression, because over the years with all the academic organizations I've worked with, when we put the newsletters online, people stopped reading them, people stopped submitting articles, the work died. The Engaged Pedagogy Association stayed with print, and they are still going.

I saw an article in the *New York Times* about a month ago or so that Kindle has peaked and now is starting to go down, and that more and more people are going back to reading books. If that's a trend, good. That's just my dinosaur impressions.

STEPHEN

As another dinosaur, I worry that this is generational. It does seem to be. And Jordan, I'd love you to weigh in on this from a different generation. The pandemic apparently has revived book sales, fairly substantially. And I—and this is a vanity thing—but I do see Ogawa's books on Instagram. And the whole Bookstagram phenomenon is enormous, and the number of people who are posting pictures of themselves with a physical book—and this is fascinating, I want to start working on this subject—these incredibly creative pictures of people with a book jacket, or a stack of books—often there are several varieties of this. But they're interacting with the physical book in a virtual space, saying "I'm reading this," or, "This is the twenty-first book I've read this week." There's a kind of an air of exaggeration to it, too. Nonetheless, there's definitely a kind of symbiosis between social media and physical books, which I think is fascinating, and it's all to the good for physical books.

JORDAN

Super, super interesting. Yeah, I'm going to go straight to Instagram after this and stalk Ogawa Yoko and see what I can find. One publication that comes to mind is *Monkey*, from Shibata Motoyuki, Meg Taylor, Roland Kelts and others. They're available on everything—print, but also Kindle and several kinds of ebooks. They're a great model. And as far as this affects *Tokyo Poetry Journal*—we're not really affected by economics, in the sense that we just choose to ignore economics. We just self-fund through our research funds and events, anyway. So we get to do whatever the hell we want. We're so irresponsible that we'll mix an Akutagawa prize-winning author with somebody that we just met in a bar, who's twenty-one years old and was tied up in bondage getting wax dripped on them in their underwear while they were doing their reading, and we think, "You belong next to an Akutagawa winner, and we will pay the publication costs for that."

BARBARA

Yes. And also, our launch parties are just fabulous. And they make us at least half what they did before the pandemic, they were making us a third of our revenue. But people would come from all different subcultures, crawling out of the woodwork.

STEPHEN

This is so beautiful, though. And so without this, to me, it feels amorphous, and I agree on *Monkey*, I read it online, but they do a beautiful print version as well. And of course, that's true for fiction now too—you know, for the books where I'm getting a royalty, I'm getting more for the audio book actually than for the print copies. But, they do every platform as well for fiction. So you can read it as an audiobook, you can read it as an online book, or you can read it as a paper copy.

JEFFREY

At Sophia University, I teach a comparative literature course, and more than half the students are reading on their *keitai*.

STEPHEN

Not even on an iPad.

JEFFREY

Well mix of iPad and *keitai*, but a mind-boggling number on *keitai*, which I can't stand to do.

STEPHEN

I'm not fond of reading on the phone but I do it. I actually do it if I'm somewhere where I don't have a book or if I have lots to read on my agenda, I keep a version on my phone.

JEFFREY

We are six minutes to the end, and we want to respect your time, Stephen. So I want to ask the most irresponsible and lazy question of the entire list and turn it over to you to see if there's anything that you'd like to add. Or to put it more precisely, what is the one question you wish interviewers would ask, but they don't? And bonus points if that question makes us look super intelligent.

STEPHEN

Another great question. I'm not sure that it'll generate bonus points, but I love it, and I've alluded to it a couple of times tonight, and it's an issue that can cut both ways. I think that no one has ever asked me about the role of editors in producing a text, whether it's poetry or prose, and getting it shepherded to print. I think a good editor is the unsung hero, for me anyway, of this entire process.

Agents actually too, in interesting ways. I have friends who are agents, and I admire what they do, even though it can be driven by other motivations. But I find editors, particularly those who work closely with texts, to be incredibly dedicated to the same kinds of things that translators are, and very invested in the service of the writer. Their names never appear anywhere, and they never get the recognition, even though they can be very involved in shaping a text. I've worked with a number of really great editors, like Stephen Shaw, who was the one who asked me to ask Murakami Ryu to cut out that chapter. But he is a wonderful man and a wonderful editor who I think is largely responsible for the great flow of brilliant titles out of Kodansha International for many, many years in the time when they were publishing a couple of dozen titles a year. I've also done projects where I sent a manuscript off not knowing who the editor was at a large house. The first I heard of it again, it was getting a review in the

New York Times or something. So having no editor, it's quicker, but much less effective. And I've spent many hours with good editors shaping texts. That's my answer.

JORDAN

Oh, beautiful. That makes us look really, really intelligent. We will claim that and rewrite it as our own question [we didn't, but that was our nefarious plan]. So, time is almost up…

JEFFREY

We hope you can make it to one of our launch parties.

STEPHEN

That would be super fun. But if not, if we could take the three of you out to dinner, that would be super fun, too. … This was just a great pleasure. I really, really love the questions. I love the conversation, thank you so much.

BARBARA

Thank you very much for your time. And I know you're very busy. And we love you dearly. We respect what you do. And we want to continue the conversation, Jeffrey, Jordan. Thank you. Lots of gratitude. Thank you so much for a beautiful interview and for this time on a really busy day.

STEPHEN

Thank you. Great meeting you, Jordan and Jeffrey.

TANYA BARNETT

REVIEWS

Factory Girls *by Arai Takako, translated by Jeffrey Angles, Jen Crawford, Carol Hayes, Rina Kikuchi, You Nakai, and Sawako Nakayasu, edited by Jeffrey Angles, Action Books, 2019*

> In the factory
> There are peculiar habits
> That is what I mean
> Peculiar habits remain here
> An old lady who spun thread
> For forty-four years here
> Still licks her index finger and twists
> Even on her deathbed
> She cannot escape the gesture
>
> (from "When the Moon Rises")

The opening poem to Arai Takako's *Factory Girls* strikes at the center of the work itself: the factory, the (female) laborer, the effect of daily life engrained upon both the modern subject and their environs. At the center stands the factory, the heart of modern industry and a lifeline that circulates throughout urban and rural centers, pumping like oxygen, economic livelihood into the homes of the working class. As noted in the editor's afterword, Arai Takako was born in Kiryū, a city in Gunma Prefecture that has long been known for its textile production (pg. 83). Arai's father manages a small weaving factory next door to the family home, and we can see that connection to the culture and industry of textiles reflected in her poetry. The same goes for the speaker(s) of her poems, who often highlight the inescapability of failing to separate work life from personal life, both within the social economy of the factory itself and the social relations that exist outside the factory. As the above poem suggests, this inescapability remains even long after the factory has long been shut down.

Factory Girls is composed of poems that were originally published in poetry journals and two of Arai's previous poetry collections, *Soul Dance* (*Tamashii dansu*) (2007) and *Beds and Looms* (*Beddo to shokki*) (2013). It is edited by Jeffrey Angles, who is himself a prolific translator of poetry and an award-winning poet. Angles, who also translates a number of the poems in this collection, is joined by fellow translators Jen Crawford, Carol Hayes, Rina Kikuchi, You Nakai, and Sawako Nakayasu. The translation is accompanied by an editor's afterword and notes on the translations, which contextualize relevant cultural and linguistic references that appear in the poems. Angles' afterword gives background information on Arai's personal history and offers insights into the themes, events, and culture that inform Arai's poetry, ranging from the collapse of the textile industry due to globalization, the moral bankruptcy of leaders in the tech sector, and the through line of nuclear devastation that runs from Hiroshima and Nagasaki all the way to Fukushima. The thoughtful decision to include an afterword in place of a translator's introduction encourages the reader to identify these themes on their own.

In terms of structure, the collection is divided into three sections titled "In the Factory", "Into the World", and "Of Gods and Small Animals". The narrative is not so much temporal as it is spatial, a proliferation of effect reverberating out from the factory like atomic energy, mirroring the impact of globalization on the working class and the environment. "Clusters of Falling Stars" calls attention to the widening schism between small, local businesses and major corporations in terms of economic wealth, and the reach of the justice system: "The dye factory Asako's father owned was put up for auction / Two months after the change in leadership / At the branch office of the bank / The rules of the free market had crushed / Local factories strangled by loans." In "Colored Glass," the speaker of the poem eats a silkworm: "There is a factory floating like an isle inside / Its head turns round and round / While blind silkworms glow / Under the colored glass window." By ruminating ("I suppose it'll stay a silkworm spitting out silk forever"), the speaker's literal consumption of the raw material for textile production to create a silk factory within her body is the ultimate act to combat the alienation of the worker from the goods of their labor. The permanence of the silkworm spinning silk in her body contrasts with the precariousness of the dye factory in "Clusters of Falling Stars," offering a stability that no longer exists in the world outside of her body.
Arai is a master of linguistic play, managing to fuse the rhythmic quality of recitation to the more concrete orthography of kanji to great effect. For example, in "For Amenouzume-san":

> Open it, that rock cave, Amenouzume-san アメノウズメさん
> Shake it, the heavens, Woman-Buried-in-the Skies 天ノ埋女さん
> Make it bloom, red cherry blossom, Forest-Sprouts-in-the-Skies 天ノ有杜芽さん

Like trying to crack a code, Arai moves through numerous combinations of homophones for the goddess, Ame no Zume, beginning with the phonetic katakana reading, アメノウズメさん , until she ultimately arrives at its sinophone reading, 天宇受売命. By brilliantly including the original Japanese for each homophone, translator Sawako Nakayasu allows the reader to follow the poem's fluctuations in meaning. In "Eh-Janaika, Eh-Janaika", the speaker ruminates on the late Edo call for revolution, "Ee ja nai ka":

> When stretched out, as in Eeeh-
> Descends the deep well of your throat
> Finds the bucket at the bottom and draws it back up
> Makes a turnabout with ja
> And then with naika, gets soaked
> That is to say
> Eh (↗), ja (↝), naika (↘)
> Forms an eternal cycle of large and small waves.

Arrows used to indicate intonation are interspersed throughout the poem, creating a visceral auditory effect, allowing us to hear the poem as we read it. In one refrain from the poem "Galapagos," Arai lists a number of words that flooded media discourse following the 2011 Great East Japan Earthquake: "Babies (*akanbō*), deceased (*hotogenkanbō*), floating (*ukabō*) on the great plain of the sea, on the verge of screaming (*orabō*), The reactor building about to fly off (*buttobō*) / Embankments (*teibō*), conspiracies (*inbō*), ministerial offices (*kanbō*) / *Unbelievabō* / *Incredibō*." Each word ends with the syllable *bō*, creating a repetition that hits relentlessly like waves striking the shore.

Arai's *Factory Girls* is frenetic, vivid, and powerful in its language and imagery. Her stories lodge themselves within your heart, which like the factory, becomes a repository for the living memories of the female laborer and all that she creates.

SIMON SCOTT

REVIEWS

Names and Rivers: Selected Poems *by Shuri Kido, ranslated by Tomoyuki Endo and Forrest Gander, Copper Canyon Press, 2022*

Shuri Kido is very much a poet of the earth and, therefore, in his poems, human experience is measured and articulated not through the historical record of human achievement—that endless rise and fall of civilisations—but through the record of geologic time, through ice ages and epochs, through continents and, most important-ly, rivers…

> In the margin, going paler and paler,
> where not even one line has been written,
> an empty sky has already collapsed.
> (After that, 500 years pass.)
> And in the second line, not yet written,
> a water rail begins to chirp.
> Where the chirp merges with the sky
> (another 300 years pass)
> a river begins,

It not so much that people or humanity are missing from his poetry (quite the op-posite), it is just a sense that humans are viewed through the long and wide lens of the land, and are, thus, seen proportionally in the deeper historical context of the earth itself—time then is marked then not by the calendar but by water and rock, by rivers… The river! As native of Morioka, or Kozukata (Kido refers to the town by its ancient name), it is no surprise rivers are a central motif in his poems—the city was built at the confluence of three rivers, the largest of which, the Kitakami, is the fourth biggest in Japan and the largest in the Tohoku region. Many Japanese cities are sliced and diced up by narrow canals (which are sometimes, aspirationally, called rivers and are good places to sit alongside and drink beer when the weather is nice), but in Morioka rivers feel like *actual* rivers—wide, long, and alive!

That is the feeling I got, anyway, when I read the cold, dripping pages of *Names and Rivers*, a collection of eighteen poems (his first in English); as well as some good commentary by Kido himself and a very insightful introduction by Tomoyuki Endo, one of the translators of the volume. The icy water which birthed these poems is very much "northern water." To my hands, it feels very different to the warmer tributaries of the Kanto region where I live—colder yet somehow more vital, more expressive of the people who live alongside it…

> In the north, water runs thin.
> So the vase you hold loses its shadow in sunlight.
> Every dream is a nightmare.
> Through this small town, ninety-five streams surge,
> and 309 bridges cross those streams.
> People come and go over them silently.
> You're someone who knows
> the secrets of the shallows and the conspiracies of the pools.

In the Afterword from *The Illusory Mother* (which is excerpted in this volume), Kido quotes Confucius (translated by Ezra Pound, of course) to express the overwhelming feeling rivers can create about our lives… "Once upon a time, Confucius, looking at a river from the bank, grieved that life 'is what passes like that, indeed, not stopping day, night'." Similarly, Kido turns to the river to measure his grief for the inevitable passing of time, but for him (unlike Confucius) it is the separation from water which speaks to the suffering of age:

> But why are riverbanks so dry?
> Being rejected by water,
> being rejected by the river,
> you idle away your life,
> and in the blink of an eye
> you've already arrived into your late years.

To be separated from water is, thus, to be separate from life itself—like the dry bank, always so close to the river, but feeling so far… The old (as long as they remember their glasses) can see clearly the pulsing force of the life which surrounds them, but it always feels at a distance, like watching your own life through the frame of the TV.

Although speaking to the liminality of our lives, Kido's poems don't leave us perpetually marooned on the sun-baked bank. Rivers are also places to be crossed and so, unsurprisingly, bridges also feature prominently in his work.

Sanma Bridge, you cross it,
hauling your lost body with you,
careful not to step through the timorous planks;
on the surface of the Kitakami River, below,
flash the red-flushed silver bellies of minnows, ayu—sweetfish—
and unborn children.

Although a measure of time, the river is also outside of it (at least outside the standard, chronological unfolding), and the future (those yet to be born) swim alongside the fishes of the present. The undead also occupy this phantom zone, this limbo…

Up there is Yugaose Bridge,
upon which, night after night, they say, a woman stands apart from
her shadow.

The river as a liminal symbol has a well-established tradition in literature and so this positioning feels familiar to us even if the terrain is not. The lost souls of past, present and future, possess the tributaries of Tohoku like they do the Styx, giving an underworld mood to Kido's lines as the dead feel as present as the living.

People die,
just as the dead die,
and then those who died twice
die three times,
and they seem to fill "afterdeath."
As such, in regions where water is abundant,
human life and death aren't separated out.

In this day and age of over-articulation, Kido's voice is refreshingly underworked yet powerful. Overall, the tone of the poems is subtle and comforting, pointing to something more without overstating it. Too often subtle notes like this are lost in translation, especially when the languages are as linguistically distant as Japanese and English, but that doesn't happen here thanks to the translators Forrest Gander and Tomoyuki Endo's masterful work. Miraculously, they manage to preserve the organic energy of the original language without leaving their own fingerprints on the pages (an all too common sin), and so the wonderfully natural lyricism of Kido's lines is allowed to remain. And it is a deep and powerful lyricism which we can feel here, yet it is not the overly emotional noise of the anguished artist crying in the night. It is deeper and more earthy, the lyricism of an echo in a mountain valley, the deep rumbling of a river… It is the sound of a good death. One where peace has been made with the land before departing its shores and crossing the River, to travel onward… To go North, until you can go no more, because "any river has its beginning and its end."

BIOS

Jeffrey Angles is a poet, translator, and professor of Japanese literature at Western Michigan University. His collection of original Japanese-language poetry won the Yomiuri Prize for Literature. Among his recent translations is Orikuchi Shinobu's modernist classic, *The Book of the Dead* (University of Minnesota Press), Itō Hiromi's "novel-in-verse" *The Thorn-Puller* (Stone Bridge Press), and Takahashi Mutsuo's book of poetry *Only Yesterday* (Canarium Books).

Aoyagi Natsumi (青柳菜摘) is an artist who completed graduate studies at Tokyo University of the Arts in 2016. Founder of the art practitioner collective and little bookshop honkbooks, in Kagurazaka, Tokyo. Recent activities include the exhibition "Logbook of a Sea Goddess" (Towada Art Center, 2022), the National Museum of Women in the Arts' Japan Committee select exhibition New Worlds (held at M5 GALLERY, 2022), the web-based project "TWO PRIVATE ROOMS – A Circle of Reading" (2020-present), the 10th Yebisu International Festival for Art & Alternative Visions (Tokyo Photographic Art Museum, 2018). Her publications include the fiction, "フジミ楼蜂" (Kotobato, vol.3, 2021), and the poetry collection, *To Quit Growing* (*Sodatsu-no-wo yameru*, 2022). http://datsuo.com/

Arai Takako (新井高子) was born in 1966 in Kiryū City, Gunma Prefecture to a family engaged in textile manufacturing, a traditional industry in Kiryū. Arai is known for writing socially engaged poetry. A frequent theme of her work is the lives of working women and the ways that they have been shaped by contemporary economic and social trends. In 2019, she represented Japan in the Iowa International Writing Program, and in 2022 at the Rotterdam International Poetry Festival. Her work has been published in English as the collection *Factory Girls* (Action Books, 2019).

Asaba Sayaka (浅葉爽香) is a chimera clad in poetry.

Shelly Bryant divides her year between Shanghai and Singapore, working as a poet, writer, and translator. She is the author of twelve volumes of poetry, a pair of travel guides, a book on classical Chinese gardens, and a short story collection. Her translations have been long-listed for the Man Asian Literary Prize in 2012, and shortlisted for the Singapore Literature Prize in 2016. You can visit Shelly's website at shellybryant.com.

Matias Chiappe Ippolito is a Professor and Researcher of Japanese literature at the Center for Asian and African Studies at El Colegio de México. He taught translation of Japanese literature at Waseda University in Tokyo, where he did his Ph.D. on the links between Japanese and Latin American literature. He has written multiple essays and accounts about life in Japan in both English and Spanish (his mother tongue). He has translated Sakaguchi Ango, Oriza Hirata and Yoshihara Sachiko, among others. Also, his professional career conceals a gruesome past that he wants to hide at all costs.

Endo Hitsuji (遠藤ヒツジ) is a poet, novelist, and spoken word artist. He is a Japan Poets Club member, and participant in the Hakuaki (白亜紀) and Shimei-tehai (指名手配) poetry groups. His own circle Yōmokusha (羊目舎) also publishes various poetry collections. Starting in 2020, along with co-host with Ito Shunta, he took on hosting of the legendary Poetry Reading Open Mic SPIRIT. In November 2020, his third poetry collection, *Along the Winding Riverbank* (*Shinaru kawagishi-ni sotte*, from Aosagi Press), received the 34th annual Fukuda Masao Prize. He was a national finalist in KOTOBA Slam Japan 2021.

Enomoto Saclaco received the Gendaishi Techo prize in 2011. Her poetry collections include *Straddling the Multiplying Eyes, Don't Take Aspirin on an Empty Stomach, Röntgen: A Submerged Flower Pot,* and *Lontano.* She lives in Saitama Prefecture and has curated a reading and talk series in Sangenjaya.

Fujita Yukihiro (藤田幸広) moved to Tokyo from Fukushima to attend Aoyama Gakuin University where he obtained his M.A. in literature in 2000. The epic poem including a play Wet Green won the Cosmos new poet encouragement prize in 2007. He has also had success translating P. B. Shelley's poetry into Japanese. His current list of publications includes a Japanese translation of *The Cenci* by P. B. Shelley (*Otohashobo-Tsurumishoten*, 2018). He currently serves as chair of the Liberal Arts Committee at Ryutsu Keizai University where he became a full professor in 2018.

Fukazawa Rena (深沢レナ) is an activist poet in Japan. Her first collection, *It Might Not Be Painful,* was published in 2017, followed by *In the Country of the Lost Things.* Her works, both essays and poems, are widely published in poetry magazines and newspapers. Her poems are anthologized in *Hidden Authors* (2017) and *The Girls in the Dark* (2018). Her third collection, *Listening to the Sea,* is forthcoming. She is a founder of the organization Don't Overlook Harassment at University, tackling sexual abuse and harassment in academia since 2020.

fukudapero (ふくだぺろ) is a poet, multi-modal anthropologist and artist residing in Kyoto, Japan. Currently a Ph.D. candidate at Ritsumeikan University, fukuda has conducted research in the UK, Rwanda and Japan. His outputs range from poetry, film, installation, photography, drawing, and novel to academic writing, exploring the boundary between art and academia, blurring and questioning them, thriving to construct a different holistic form of knowledge. His recent works include the short film *Sitting, Gazing, Gazed* (2020), the poetry collection *flowers like blue glass* (2018) and *the installation yoyo* (im/pulse exhibition, Kyoto City University of Arts Art Gallery @KCUA, 2018). Winner of Best Experimental Film at the Manchester International Film Festival 2016 (*o —a film shot with water lens–*), fukuda was nominated for the Forward Prize for Poetry 2020 and chosen for the emerging poets selection 2020 by *Gendai-shi Techo* magazine. www.fukudapero.com

Fuzuki Yumi (文月悠光) was born in 1991 in Hokkaido, Japan. Began writing at the age of 10, and at sixteen was awarded the Gendai-shi Techo Prize. Her final year in high school, Fuzuki's first published collection, *In this Suitable World, This Unsuitable Me* (*Tekisetsu-na sekai no tekisetsu-narazaru watashi*, 2009) was awarded the Nakahara Chūya Prize, and has also been published in Finnish translation. At age eighteen, she was awarded the Maruyama Yutaka Memorial Modern Poetry Prize (2010). Other books include *Deeper than the Roof* (*Yane-yori fukabuka-to*, from Shichosha), *Our Cat* (*Watashi-tachi no neko*, from Nanaroku), a book of essays, *Diary of Baptism* (*Senrei dairii*, from Poplar), *Mousey Poets, Take to the Streets* (*Okubyō-na shijin, machi-he deru*, from Shichosha). Gives many poetry readings, and holds poetry exhibitions and collaborations with musicians and other artists. Her most recent volume is *Like Parallel Worlds* (*Parareru waarudo-no you na mono*, from Shichosha).

Andrew Gebert is a Tokyo-based translator, researcher, and gentleman farmer.

Matthew Guay is an Associate Professor at Ryutsu Keizai University in the greater Tokyo area. He is an American national who loves learning languages and is currently building fluency in his fifth, the endangered Yaeyaman language spoken on Ishigaki and the surrounding Yaeyaman Archipelago. He received his M.A. in translation studies from the University of Birmingham in 2019 focusing on poetry translation between unrelated languages and began his Ph.D. at Kyushu University in descriptive and anthropological linguistics focusing on Ryukyuan languages in 2022. In addition to research, he also enjoys teaching and adapted his methods into a textbook he coauthored, published by National Geographic Learning/Cengage called *Free Talking*. He is a father of two, fronts the Tokyo-based indie rock band The Oversleep Excuse on the Ricco label, and referees games in his children's local football league on the weekends.

Judy Halebsky is a poet and scholar. She is the author of *Spring and a Thousand Years (Unabridged)* (University of Arkansas Press, 2020), *Tree Line* (New Issues 2014) and *Sky=Empty*, winner of the New Issue Prize (New Issues, 2010). She has also published articles on cultural translation and noh theatre. She is a professor of Literature and Language at Dominican University of California and the director of the MFA program.

Kawaguchi Harumi (川口晴美) is a poet born in Obama City, Fukui Prefecture. She graduated from Waseda University's Faculty of Letters, majoring in literature. Her poetry collections include *Hantō no chizu* (Map of the Peninsula, 10th Kenkichi Yamamoto Literary Award), *Tiger is Here* (46th Jun Takami Award), and *Yagate majo no mori ni naru* (*Soon it will be a witch's forest*, 30th Sakutaro Hagiwara Award). She supervised the Japan-Australia bilingual anthology *YorokoBI-KuruSHIMI-HirugaeRU shi pleasant troubles* (translated by Rina Kikuchi, 2018).

Kendall Heitzman is an associate professor of Japanese literature at the University of Iowa. His translation of Furukawa Hideo's "The Little Woods in Fukushima" appears in *Monkey* Vol. 3 (2022), and his translation of Fujino Kaori's *Nails and Eyes* is forthcoming from Pushkin Press. He has also translated stories and essays by Shibasaki Tomoka, Nakagami Nori, and Takiguchi Yōshō.

Jeffrey Johnson did his doctoral work at UW Seattle and teaches comparative literature and translation in Tokyo. He spent his 20s in Arizona, his early 30s in Barcelona, and is now a long time resident of Tokyo. He is the author of two books of criticism: *Bakhtinian Theory in Japanese Studies* (Mellen), and *Haiku Poetics in 20th Century Avant-Garde Poetry* (Lexington), and a founding editor of the *Tokyo Poetry Journal*.

Katayama Sayuri (片山さゆ里) is a musician and poet, born in 1990 in Toyama Prefecture. Starting in 2013, she began performing live solo music shows, accompanying her original lyrics on folk guitar, and her performances are known for their emotional, personal overflowings that frequently leave her audiences sobbing. In 2021 she won the West Tokyo Slam of KOTOBA Slam Japan, and went on to the national finals, where she was selected for the Translator's Prize, which includes a feature in *Tokyo Poetry Journal*. December 2022 saw the release of her eponymous CD *Songs of Katayama Sayuri* ③.

Rina Kikuchi is a poetry translator, a professor of literature at Shiga University, Japan, and an adjunct Associate Professor of poetry in the Faculty of Arts and Design at the University of Canberra. She is currently working on a bilingual anthology of contemporary Japanese women poets with Jen Crawford, a collaborative poetry translation project of Misaki Takako's poetry, and a research project on Japanese women's poetry of the Asia Pacific War. Her books of poetry translations include *Poet to Poet: Contemporary Women Poets from Japan* (RWP, 2017, co-edited with Jen Crawford) and *Pleasant Troubles* (RWP, 2018, co-edited with Harumi Kawaguchi). She was a residential fellow of Writers Immersion and Cultural Exchange, WRICE, at RMIT in 2021.

Miho Kinnas, a 2019 Pushcart Prize nominee, is a Japanese poet & author living on Hilton Head Island, South Carolina, where she conducts poetry workshops and operates a community bookshop, An Island Bookshelf. She is the author of two poetry collections: *Today, Fish Only* and *Move Over, Bird* (Math Paper Press). She holds an MFA in creative writing (poetry) from City University of Hong Kong.

Kisaka Ryo (木坂涼) was born in 1958 in Saitama Prefecture, Japan. She published her first collection of poems, *Jikan wa jibun to* (Time Tells Me) in 1981. Her second book of poetry with the onomatopoeic title *Tsut-Tsut-To* was awarded the Hanatsubaki Poetry Prize. *Konjiki no ami (The Golden Net)* published in 1996, won that year's Japanese Art Prize. Kisaka has written numerous books for children, including the Roly-Poly Family series and the popular Bento Hug picture book. She is also a prolific translator of children's literature. Works by Margaret Wise Brown, William Steig, Simms Taback, Lauren Child and many others speak to Japanese children through Kisaka.

Koori Hironobu (コオリヒロノブ) has been active as a performance poet since 2003. In 2006, he took part in a Japanese poetry competition known as "Poetry Boxing." In 2020, he produced a journal titled *unedited*. In 2021, he participated in his first slam, and made it through the Fukuoka Regional Slam to the National Finals of KOTOBA Slam Japan, which he won and went on to represent Japan at the Poetry World Cup in Paris.

Eric Margolis is a writer, editor, and translator from Japanese based in Nagoya. His fiction, poetry, and literary translations have been published in *Metropolis Magazine, River River, Eclectica,* and the *Yale Journal of Literary Translation*. His nonfiction has appeared in *The New York Times, The Japan Times, Foreign Policy, Vox, Slate,* and elsewhere. He recently published a novel, *The Golden State,* and can be found on Twitter @ericdmargolis.

Michiyama Rain (道山れいん): After graduating from the University of Tokyo Department of Japanese Literature, Rain published three volumes of poetry while working as a creative director in video, music, and language arts. Hailing from Japan's southern island of Kyushu, Fukuoka Prefecture, Rain's beloved Omuta is known both for an awesome local dialect and as home of UNESCO World Heritage Coal Mines. This forms the base of his poetry, which mines an intensely personal trove of memory, seeking to strike a universal vein to connect with people around the world and foster mutual faith. 2017 National Finalist in Poetry Slam Japan; 2019, first Japanese recipient of the Poetry Video Prize from Finland's Lahti Poetry Marathon. and 2022 Kotoba Slam Japan National Champion.

Taylor Mignon is a poet, editor, translator, and lecturer. He teaches a Kenneth Rexroth seminar at Rikkyo University and Creative Writing at Keio and Musashi universities. In *Kyoto Journal* #86, he is named as someone who "brings people together, creates events that showcase creativity and give rise to more creativity…." His poetry was described in the *Japan Times* as "steeped in the avant-garde, yet surprisingly palatable." He coedited *Poesie Yaponesia: A Bilingual Anthology* (Printed Matter Press, 2000), coedited and co-translated *Distant Frogs: Selected Senryu* by Gengorō (The Hokuseido Press, 2007). He led the translation and editing of *Bearded Cones & Pleasure Blades: The Collected Poems of Torii Shōzō* (highmoonoon, 2013). His newest book as editor is *VOU: Visual Poetry Tokio* (1958-1978), (Isobar Press, 2022). His translations are included in an anthology of 20th century Japanese experimental poetry (New Directions, 2022).

Minesawa Noriko (峯澤典子) is a poet who resides around Kichijoji in Tokyo. Chosen for the Eureka Newcomer Prize (Yuriika Shinnin) by poet Hisaki Matsuura in 2008. Her collections include *Mizu Hanga* (Furansudo), *Hikari No Tojo De* (Shichigatsudo), and *Ano Toki Fuyu No Kodomotachi* (Shichigatsudo). Managed the *Gendaishi Techo* poetry review in 2018. Find her on Twitter @noriko_minesawa or follow her blog at https://note.com/unjourunpoeme.

Misumi Mizuki (三角みづ紀) was born in Kagoshima in 1981, and now lives in Sapporo. She received the Modern Poetry Journal Prize while still in college, and her later prizes include the Nakahara Chūya Award for *Overkill*, her first book of poetry, the Southern Japan Literature Award, and the Rekitei New Voice Award for her second collection *Kanashiyaru (Beloved)*, and the Hagiwara Sakutarō Award for her fifth book, the original Japanese version of the collection, *Rooms With No Neighbors (Rinjin no inai heya*, trasnalAndrew Gebert's English translation by *Tokyo Poetry Journal* Excursions imprint in 2022), the outcome of a one-month trip through Europe. She regularly gives readings in and outside Japan. *Cakes You Can Find Anywhere*, her eighth book of poetry, came out in August 2020.

Miyao Setsuko (宮尾節子) is a poet. Her poem "Ashita sensō ga hajimaru" (Tomorrow the war begins) was originally posted on SNS in 2014 and became a topic of conversation in various media due to its explosive spread. She has published several poetry collections, including *Dosutoefusukī no aozora (Dostoevsky's blue sky*, 2005), *Ashita sensō ga hajimaru (Tomorrow the war begins*, 2014), *Onna ni kike (Ask a woman*, 2019), and *Gyūnyū take (Milk mountain)*, among others. She hosts a linked poetry series on Twitter. She was also the recipient of the La Mer Prize for Contemporary Poetry of 1993.

Moriyama Megumi (森山恵) is a Tokyo-born poet, English haiku poet, and translator. She is the author of four full-length books of poetry, including *Tangible Dreams (Yume no tezawari*, 2005), which was composed for a choir piece and published. Moriyama had been selected as a New Poet by *Gendaishi Techo* and her poems have appeared in numerous journals and anthologies. She has recently co-translated the full text of Arthur Waley's *The Tale of Genji* and has won the 2020 Donald Keene Special Award. Her latest work is the translation of Virginia Woolf's *The Waves* into Japanese.

Nagae Yūki (永方佑樹) is a poet and performance artist. She received the 2012 Poetry and Thought Newcomer's Award; her 2019 poetry collection *Fuzai toshi* [Absentee Cities] was awarded the Rekitei Prize. Her most recent project is GeoPossession, in which 3D audio recordings of writers reading from their work in specific locations around Tokyo are made available to listeners at those locations. She has performed at the Saint-Remi Museum in Reims, France, and across Japan, and is a lecturer at Nagoya University of the Arts. Participated in the International Writing Program (IWP) at the University of Iowa in fall 2022, funded by the Bureau of Educational and Cultural Affairs at the U.S. Department of State.

Nakagawa Junnosuke earned his MA in TESOL at the Graduate School of Humanities at Josai International University. A passionate and supportive teacher who has taught English to primary school students, he enjoys exploring strategies to develop students' communication skills and motivation to learn English. Also, a researcher who has investigated the impact of online learning environments on Japanese EFL university students' communication skills, views, challenges, and preferences. Studied at Camosun College, Victoria, Canada. He loves playing soccer, growing plants, eating, and traveling.

Martha Nakamura was awarded the Gendaishi Techō Prize in 2016. In 2018, her debut poetry collection *Tanuki Box* won the Nakahara Chōya Prize, and in 2020, she became the youngest person ever to win the Hagiwara Sakutarō Prize for her follow-up collection, *The Lighthouse That Calls Down Rain*. In 2021, she was honored by Waseda University with the Tsubouchi Shōyō Encouragement Award, given only once every two years.

Zoria Petkoska K. is a polyglot, polymath, and poet. Or simply, a curious cat. Holds undergraduate and Master's degrees in English Literature and Translation, with postgraduate research studies in Japanese visual poetry from TUFS. Edits and writes for several outlets, both travel journalism and poetry. Published her first poetry book when she was ten years old, and writes and reads in English, Macedonian, and sometimes Japanese. Zoria is a neo-Tokyoite telling stories about the city in many forms. She loves all the things you would expect—travel, coffee, cyberpunk, concrete walls, power lines, the rattle of trains in the distance.

Sakisaki Kujira (向坂くじら) formed the electric guitar and poetry unit Anti-Trench in 2016, together with Gt. Kumagai Yuya. She has appeared on TBS Radio After 6 Junction. In 2022, *Totemo chiisana rikai no tame-ni (For the Sake of a Very Small Understanding)* was published by Shironeko-sha. Active as an educator, she teaches Japanese language and literature in Okegawa City, Saitama, innovating new programs that were covered in the *Asahi Shimbun* newspaper and elsewhere. She works to keep poetry workshops, classes and other events going in many educational and community support centers while continuing her studies and research in education. Her English translations were also featured in *TPJ*'s volume 9.

San Simon (サンシ・モン) might be something like a poet with a guitar. He's interested in words and is honored to have his words translated into English, to see what fruits his Japanese words will bear in English. Let's talk about poetry together. National finalist in KOTOBA Slam Japan.

Simon Scott originates from Christchurch, New Zealand and is a Kamakura-based freelance journalist, writer and poet who has been published in a very diverse range of international newspapers, magazines and literary journals. He is currently working on a master's thesis through the University of Auckland about the Beat Generation, East Asia and Buddhism.

Eric Selland has translated Modernist and contemporary Japanese poets for forty years. He is editor of an anthology of Japanese Modernist and avant-garde poetry with poet and translator Sawako Nakayasu, which is scheduled to appear in 2024. His translations include *The Day Laid Bare* by Kiwao Nomura and *Kusudama* by Minoru Yoshioka (both on Isobar Press). Eric has translated a number of contemporary novels as well, including *The Guest Cat* by Takashi Hiraide. He has a book of visual poetry in the works, expected to be available this spring.

Shiraishi Setsuhi (白石雪妃) is a Tokyo-based calligraphy artist pursuing the beauty of lines and spaces that influence the viewers momentarily. Her calligraphy is a comprehensive art, often created in collaborations with other arts in a unique style while transmitting the world of traditional calligraphy. She designed the concept of the new uniform for the 2014 FIFA World Cup Japan National Team, "Circle." She worked on an installation for the Japan Pavilion event at Expo Milan and performed at the 21st Century Museum of Contemporary Art, Kanazawa. She has been an invited artist at Abiko International Outdoor Art Exhibition Installation, and has done solo exhibitions in Paris, NY, SF, JICC Embassy of Japan in the United States, live tours in six cities in the United States, and was also invited overseas to France every year.

Shibuya Gokai (渋谷剛海) is a graduate student in English education at Josai International University. He would like to tell future children in Japan about the fun of languages through teaching English and literature. He sees translation as not just an exchange, but a blending process, so the resulting translations can be read as something with nuw colors.

Jordan A. Y. Smith is a producer for Naro.tv, writer, researcher, and translator living between Tokyo and Los Angeles. Co-founder of the poetry-technology collective Cōem, producing the 3D audio hologram project GeoPossession (2022). Author of poetry and art volume *Syzygy* (Awai Books, 2020), and co-author of *Sea of Trees*, and *√IC: Redux*. Co-founder of KOTOBA, the national poetry slam of Japan. Producer for BBC Radio programs on Japanese poetry and culture, and translator of many of Japan's leading poets. Curator for DIESEL Art Gallery (Shibuya). After completing a Ph.D. in Comparative Literature at UCLA, he served as Associate Professor at Josai International University, and taught comparative literature, Japanese studies, and translation at UCLA, Waseda, Sophia, CSU Long Beach. Instagram @jordangiraffe

Melinda Smith is a poet who lives and writes on Ngunnawal and Ngambri country, Canberra, Australia. She also holds a Bachelor of Japanese Studies with Honours from the ANU. She has been working with Rina Kikuchi to translate Japanese women's poetry since the 2017 Poetry on the Move festival. Her translations of Kawaguchi Harumi, Misumi Mizuki, and others have appeared in the 2017 Recent Work Press *Poet to Poet* anthology and in her own book *Man-handled* (2020). She participated in the series of translation workshops and readings organised by Rina in Japan in 2018, and her own poems were translated into Japanese for the *Pleasant Troubles* anthology (2018). She has also translated poems from Russian and Latin, and her own poems have been rendered in Chinese, Italian and Burmese.

Stephen Snyder serves as Vice President for Academic Affairs and Dean of Language Schools at Middlebury College. He has translated works by Ogawa Yōko, Ōe Kenzaburō, Miri Yu, Kirino Natsuo, and Murakami Ryū, among others. His translation of Ogawa's *The Memory Police* was a finalist for the 2019 National Book Award for Translated Literature and for the International Booker Prize. He chaired the selection panel for the National Book Award for Translated Literature in 2021.

Sonic Nurse (そにっくなーす) was born March 28, 1989 in Saitama, Japan and began writing poetry in middle school. In addition to doing poetry readings, she writes novels and composes songs to accompany her singing on guitar. In civilian life, she's an outpatient psychiatric nurse, which puts her in touch with every aspect of language and human existence, as she herself struggles through daily life. She writes poems when she's going through tough times, and ideally does so on a fast train. Three-time national finalist in Kotoba Slam Japan, she's excited to get her poetry out globally.

Keijiro Suga (管啓次郎) is a poet and professor of critical theory in the graduate program Places, Arts, and Consciousness at Meiji University. Author of eight collections of poetry in Japanese and a chapbook in English, *Transit Blues*, he has been invited to read at poetry festivals and universities in more than twenty countries. He is also a prolific translator from English, French, and Spanish to Japanese. His most recent translations are Edouard Glissant's *Le quatrième siècle* (2019) and *M Train* by Patti Smith (2020).

Barbara Summerhawk is *ToPoJo*'s Editor Emeritus. In 2010, she won the Golden Crown Literary Award for best anthology for *Sparkling Rain: Fiction From Women Who Love Women* in Japan. Her poetry and fiction has been published in *The Spirit that Moves Us, Poet and Critic, Printed Matter*, and many anthologies. She holds a 7th *dan* in aikido and teaches in her dojo in Nishi Tokyo. She always looks forward to getting through the middle of next Tuesday.

Ayako Takahashi is a scholar and translator teaching at University of Hyogo in Japan. Her recent scholarship includes the books *Ambience: Ecopoetics in the Anthropocene* (Shichosha, 2022) and *Reading Gary Snyder* (Shichosha 2018). She has published translations of many American poets such as Jane Hirshfield, Anne Waldman, and Joanne Kyger, among others (*Anthology of Contemporary American Women Poets*, Shichosha 2012).

Takahashi Mutsuo (高橋睦郎) is one of Japan's most prominent living poets, having won almost every major poetry prize in the nation. Since first attracting the attention of the Japanese literary world with his bold poetic evocations of homoerotic desire in the 1960s, Takahashi has published nearly fifty books of poetry, essays, literary criticism, and other work. Several collections of English translations of his poetry are available, including *Poems of a Penisist* (University of Minnesota Press, 2012), *Sleeping, Sinning, Falling* (City Lights, 1992), and *Only Yesterday* (Canarium, 2023). His memoir *Twelve Views from the Distance* (University of Minnesota Press, 2012), translated by Jeffrey Angles, was shortlisted for a Lambda Literary Award.

Tanaka Ikuko (1937 -2021) lived in Okayama prefecture in western Japan. She was a member of the Japan Poets Association. *The Song of Rowanberry*, her sixth collection of poems, was awarded the Ono Juzaburo Prize and the Chu-shikoku Regional Poetry Prize. In 2015, her works were included in a prestigious contemporary poetry collection curated by Shichōsha.

Tōma Hiroko (トーマ・ヒロコ) is a poet from Urasoe City in the southern region of Okinawa Main Island. Tōma made her debut in 2007 in a short anthology, 1999, that she and her friends produced after graduating together from Okinawa International University. Two years later, she received the 32nd Yamanokuchi Baku Poetry Prize for her solo anthology, *Hitori karendā* (My personal calendar). In 2019, she published *Pasta o maku* (I wind spaghetti). Tōma regularly showcases her work in local venues in Okinawa, sometimes in collaboration with calligraphic artwork created by her mother, and most recently alongside her own photography.

Wago Ryoichi (和合亮一) is a poet and high school Japanese literature teacher from Fukushima city, Japan. In 2017, the French translation of his book, *Pebbles of Poetry*, won the Nunc Magazine award for best foreign-language poetry collection. Since March 2011, his writing has focused on the ecological devastation of the areas affected by the Tohoku earthquake, tsunami and the nuclear meltdown of the Fukushima Daiichi power station. His poem "Abandoned Fukushima" is sung by choirs across Japan as a prayer for hope and renewal.

Yamazaki Shūhei (山崎修平) is a Tokyo-based poet and novelist. His 2020 poetry collection, *Dance Eat Sleep*, won the Rekitei Newcomer's Prize. His debut novel, *The Sweet Smell of Teegebäck*, has just been published by Kawade Shobō.

Yotsumoto Yasuhiro (四元康祐) was born in Osaka, Japan in 1959, and grew up in Hiroshima. He has published fifteen books of poetry and two full length novels. The most recent publication is *Swallowed by a Dragon, Swallowed a Dragon*, a collection of essays and poems on Europe. Books in English translation include *Family Room* (tr. by the author), *Poems of Minashita Kiryu, Yotsumoto Yasuhiro & Soh Sakon* (tr. by Leith Morton), and *Starboard of My Wife* (tr. by Takako Lento), all published from Vagabond Press. Yasuhiro is also active in translation and literary criticism. After spending thirty-four years in the US and Germany, Yasuhiro came back to Japan in 2020, where he lectures in several universities and organizes poetry events called Poetry Talks Live based at Hikari no uma, a live house in Tokyo.

Victoria Young is the Kawashima Assistant Professor in Japanese Literature and Culture at the Faculty of Asian and Middle Eastern Studies, University of Cambridge, and a Fellow of Selwyn College. Her work engages with issues of multilinguality, historical memory, and translation in Japanese literature, in particular as these are articulated in fiction by Okinawan, ethnic Korean, and 'trans-border' writers. She is writing a monograph on the role of translation in constructing the borders of contemporary Japanese literature. Her translation of Tōma Hiroko's poem "Backbone" (Senaka) can be found in Davinder L. Bhowmik and Steve Rabson, *Islands of Protest: Japanese Literature from Okinawa* (Honolulu: University of Hawai'i Press, 2016).

ACKNOWLEDGMENTS

Certain poems from this issue have first appeared in the following publications:

Endo Hitsuji, 『遠藤ヒツジ詩集：しなる川岸に沿って』.

Takahashi Mutsuo, *Tsui kinō no koto* (Tokyo: Shichōsha, 2018).

Tōma Hiroko, "Translation" first published as *Hon'yaku* in her first solo anthology, *Hitori karendā*, 2009). "For the Peacemakers" first published as *Heiwa o tsukuru monotachi ni* in the May 2022 issue of *Christa* magazine.

The selection of poems from *Kūki no nikki*, by Kawaguchi Harumi, Arai Takako, Miyao Setsuko, Jordan A. Y. Smith, and Yotsumoto Yasuhiro, are taken from 空気の日記 (Diary of the Air or Air Diaries), published online by *Spinner*, the journal associated with Omotesando Spiral, in a series curated and produced by Matsuda Tomoharu (https://spinner.fun/diary/). The premise was that twenty-three poets would take turns writing one poem per day for one full year, beginning with the onset of the coronavirus "stay at home" restrictions in Japan. It was later published as a book with the same title by Kankanbou (2022).

Fuzuki Yumi, *Parareru waarudo no youna mono* (Tokyo: Shichōsha, 2022).